CHEKHOV THE MAN

A. P. CHEKHOV

CHEKHOV THE MAN

by
KORNEI CHUKOVSKY

Translated from the Russian
by PAULINE ROSE

HASKELL HOUSE PUBLISHERS Ltd.
Publishers of Scarce Scholarly Books
NEW YORK, N. Y. 10012
1974

HASKELL HOUSE PUBLISHERS Ltd.

Publishers of Scarce Scholarly Books

280 LAFAYETTE STREET

NEW YORK, N. Y. 10012

Library of Congress Cataloging in Publication Data

Chukovskii, Kornei Ivanovich, 1882–1969.
    Chekhov the man.

    Reprint of the 1945 ed. published by Hutchinson,
London.
    1. Chekhov, Anton Pavlovich, 1860–1904.
I. Title.
PG3458.C52 1974   891.7'2'3 [B]   74–6384
ISBN 0–8383–1867–3

Printed in the United States of America

CHAPTER ONE 49817

I

CROESUS COULD NOT HAVE BEEN MORE HOSPITABLE. HOSPITABILITY was a veritable passion with him. He had hardly settled down in a village than he immediately began inviting throngs of guests to stay with him. To many this might have seemed madness: here was a man just emerged from the financial straits in which he had been for many years; he was still hard put to it to support his family—his mother, brother, sister and father; he did not have a penny saved for the morrow; yet he filled his house to overflowing with people whom he dined and wined and doctored.

Once he rented a country house in an out-of-the-way Ukrainian provincial hole. He had not even seen it; he had no idea what it was like, yet he lost no time in inviting all sorts of people from Moscow, from St. Petersburg, from Nizhni-Novgorod.

As for his house outside Moscow, it was like a hotel.

"They slept on the sofas, several people in each room," his brother, Mikhail, recalls. "They even slept in the passage. Writers, young women, local land department officials, country doctors, distant relatives"—the invited and uninvited would crowd his home for weeks at a time.

But even this was not enough for him.

"We're expecting Ivanenko. Svobodin is coming. I'm going to invite Barantsevich. Of course Suvorin will be here . . ." he wrote to Nata Lintvareva from Melikhovo in 1892.

And in the same breath he invited her as well. The letters that followed showed that, in addition to these five people, he also invited Lazarev-Gruzinsky, Yezhov and Leikin, to say nothing of Levitan, who had already arrived!

Nine guests—but that was not all. His home provided constant shelter for people who were not even considered visitors: friends of the family, "permanent guests", and swarms of incidental, nameless folk.

Needless to say, he often suffered from having so many people about him.

"I've had guests, guests, and more guests here, ever since Good Friday . . . and I haven't written a single line." But even this could not suppress his uncontrollable passion for company.

5

His invitations were extended gaily, spiritedly, playfully, intriguingly, their very style reflecting the atmosphere of youthful merriment that surrounded him.

For instance, he wrote to the editor of the weekly, *Sever* (North): "As you've published my portrait and thereby helped me to acquire fame, I want to present you with five bunches of radishes from my very own garden. But you've got to come down here" (from St. Petersburg —four hundred miles away!—K.C.) "to eat those radishes."

His invitation to the architect Shekhtel read:

"If you don't turn up I hope your braces come undone in public, right in the middle of the street."

And to the vaudeville writer Bilibin he wrote:

"Now here's what you ought to do: get yourself a wife and come and stay with us for a week or two. I promise you'll become a magnificent prize idiot."

What is of interest is not so much Chekhov's hospitality as that tremendous vital energy of his, which was reflected in this hospitality.

When inviting his friends and acquaintances to visit him, he described the pleasures that awaited them in the most superlative terms, as though he were writing advertisements for health resorts:

"It is a very healthy spot, with lots of gaiety, plenty of food and people galore. . . A hundred times warmer and more beautiful than the Crimea. . . A comfortable carriage, very tolerable horses, a marvellous road, and people who are first-rate in all respects. . . Wonderful bathing. . ."

He was very insistent when extending an invitation, and would not brook even the thought of a refusal.

"I'll get you down here if I have to lasso you," he wrote to the writer Shcheglov. That is what most of his invitations really were— lassos, so forcefully did they reflect his persistent, irresistible will.

In his passion for inviting people he was often indiscriminate. He invited every Tom, Dick and Harry as though every one of them was vitally necessary for him, whether it was the tiresome, noisy braggart Gilyarovsky, or the insignificant Yezhov, who was always taking offence.

Among all the men of letters whom I can recall there is not one who can stand comparison with Chekhov as regards his sweeping, generous hospitality. Its grand style was much more in keeping with the owner of a large estate than with this grandson of a peasant and son of a misérable shopkeeper. Yet in a dozen years not a single large estate saw, under its ancient limes, such a higgledy-piggledy parade of diverse visitors as that which was a daily phenomenon at squalid, shabby Melikhovo.

II

This passion for having lots of people about him remained with Chekhov to the end of his days.

When, already in the last stages of tuberculosis, he paid a short visit to Moscow, so many people kept coming to his flat that he did not have a free moment from morning until night.

"There was always someone at his place during the day," Nemirovich-Danchenko recalls, and proceeds to remark on something that struck him as incredibly odd: "He didn't seem to be in the least exhausted by all this, or at any rate he gladly resigned himself to being exhausted."

If, when tuberculosis had finally undermined his energy, he "didn't seem to be in the least exhausted" by the endless string of visitors who kept coming to him with their worries from sunrise to sunset, then what must he have been like in his younger days, when, with an avidity almost like that of insatiable hunger, he hurled himself upon more and more new people, at the same time displaying a sociability the like of which, apparently, no other person had ever possessed!

Unusually quick in making friends and acquaintances, Chekhov, during his first years in Moscow, came literally to know the entire city, all strata of Moscow society. At the same time he studied Moscow's suburbs—Babkino and Chikino, and Voskresensk and Zvenigorod, ravenously gulping down all the impressions of the life about him.

And that is why in the letters of his earlier years we constantly read:

"I've just been to the races. . . Slept and ate and drank with the officers. . . I often drop in on the monks. . . I'm going to visit a glass factory. . . Am going to take a trip through the Ukraine for the whole summer and will visit the fairs à la Nozdrev. . . I drank and sang with two opera basses. . . I often call at the court of justice. . . Was in a stinking pub where I saw two rogues playing billiards in a billiard-room that was packed full. . . I acted as best man for a certain doctor. . . Bogemsky is paying slight court to Yadenka, and also visits Ludmilochka. Levitan is leading the life of a gay dog. Olga is sorry she hasn't married Matvei. . . Nelly has arrived and is going hungry. . . The baroness has given birth" . . . and so on.

Without this phenomenal sociability of his, without his constant readiness to hobnob with anyone at all, to sing with singers and get drunk with drunkards, without that burning interest in the lives, habits, conversations and occupations of hundreds and thousands of people, he would certainly never have been able to create that colossal, encyclopedically detailed Russian world of the eighties and nineties of the past century, which goes by the name of Chekhov's *Short Stories*.

If all the people portrayed in the many-volumed collection of Chekhov's *Short Stories*—all his policemen, midwives, actors, tailors, prisoners, cooks, religious devotees, teachers, prostitutes, landowners, bishops, circus performers, functionaries of all ranks and departments, peasants from northern and from southern regions, generals, bathhouse attendants, engineers, horse-thieves, monastery novices, merchants, singers, soldiers, match-makers, piano-tuners, firemen, examining judges, deacons, professors, shepherds, lawyers—if all of these could, in some miraculous way, come streaming forth from his books out into a Moscow street, what a terrific mob they would make! —even the largest square could not hold such a crowd. Compared to Chekhov with his multitude of characters other writers seem empty, so relatively few are the people to be found in every hundred pages of their works.

It is difficult to believe that all these crowds of people who populate Chekhov's books were created by one man, that only two eyes and not a thousand saw with such superhuman keenness, remembered and portrayed for all time, those countless gestures, gaits, smiles, countenances; difficult to believe that it was not a thousand hearts, but only one which embraced all the pains and joys of that host of people.

And what a good time he had with people! With those whom he liked, of course. And he found no difficulty in liking anyone, for although he was mercilessly sarcastic and apparently saw through everyone, yet when he first met a person he was almost invariably naively trusting, and the generosity of his heart was so limitless that he was ready to ascribe to the most miserable creatures the riches of his own personality. That is why we so often read, in his letters:

"A delightful fellow", "a darling man", "a splendid chap", "a likable and remarkably gifted person", "a dear, good-natured little creature", "a wonderful warm-hearted family and I've become very much attached to them", "a marvellous creature who's extremely good, and so meek", "she's every whit as nice as her brothers, who just fascinate me", "he's a brick and not without talent", "such an attractive woman, the like of whom it's hard to find", and so on.

What, for instance, do you care about the owner of the summer villa which you rent for the few warm months of the year? The summer goes by, you return to the city and forget about him for all time. But all Chekhov had to do was to rent a place in the south from some people by the name of Lintvarev, whom he had never set eyes on before, and he straightaway assured you that all the Lintvarevs—there were six of them—were dear people, and for many years he included the whole family in his circle of close friends or, as he put it, "he lit an inextinguishable *lampada**" before this family.

The same could be said of the Kiselev family, from whom he rented his cottage near Moscow for three years in succession. He became friendly not only with them but with their children, their relatives and their guests.

He was on equally close terms with all the editors who happened to publish his works, even with Vukol Lavrov and Sablin, not to mention Alexei Suvorin.

Chekhov was such a gregarious creature that he even contemplated writing in collaboration with others, and he was ready to invite the most unsuitable people as his collaborators.

"Look here, Korolenko. Let's work together. We'll write a play. Four acts. We'll do it in a fortnight."

This, in spite of the fact that Korolenko had never written any plays and had absolutely nothing to do with the theatre.

And to Bilibin:

"Let's write a vaudeville sketch in two acts. You make up the first act and I'll do the second. We'll split the royalties."

And to Suvorin:

"Let's write a tragedy—*Holofernes*—based on the opera *Judith*. We'll make Judith fall in love with Holofernes. . . There are any number of subjects. We can write a *Solomon*, or one about Napoleon III and Eugenie, or Napoleon I at Elba."

And to Suvorin again, several years later:

"Let's write a couple of short stories. . . You do the beginnings, I the end."

He was even ready to write a play with Goltsev, a professor of law and a man seemingly totally unsuited for writing fiction. "I bet you we could do it if only you wanted to. I know we could. Think it over."

The desire of this great master to co-operate with anyone, even the most insignificant writer, was no affectation, for he gladly undertook such collaboration at the first opportunity.

Shchepkina-Kupernik recalls:

"Once Chekhov suggested writing a one-act play with me and even wrote the first monologue for it, a long one."

When Suvorin accepted Chekhov's proposal and agreed to collaborate to write a play, Chekhov rolled up his sleeves and with his

---

* A light that is always kept lit before an ikon.—K.C.

usual energy got down to work immediately, and in his next letter he worked out, in detail, all the ten characters for the play. It was certainly not his fault if the undertaking fell through shortly after.

In his travels he was also free with his invitations. He suggested going to Persia with Suvorin's son, to Africa with Maxim Kovalevsky, to the Volga with Potapenko, and to the Don steppes with Pleshcheyev.

"As regards making a trip to Babkino during Shrovetide, the decision of my whole gang of bandits is: Go!" he wrote to Alexei Kiselev.

"If we got together a large crowd and went abroad, we could do it very cheaply," he suggested in a letter to his sister.

He liked working with people and roaming about with them, but best of all he liked to have a good time with people playing pranks and cracking jokes with them.

"We went riding with a four-in-hand in grandfather's carriage on Thursday," he wrote Pleshcheyev from Sumy at the end of the 'eighties. "We laughed a lot and had heaps of adventures, misunderstandings, stops, and meetings on the way. . . If you had only been with us and could have seen our angry coachman, Roman; you couldn't look at him without laughing. . . We ate and drank every half hour and laughed till our sides ached. . . After a warm pleasant meeting with someone we would all go off into screams of laughter without any reason at all, and every evening after that we were certain to laugh without stopping."

However, there was sufficient reason for the hilarity—it was Chekhov himself. He had been endowed with such a large dose of this youthful, immortal mirth that no sooner did he have a free moment in the middle of his extremely hard work than laughter just flowed out of him and it was impossible not to laugh with him. He would don a Bokhara kimono, blacken his face with soot, put on a turban and play the Bedouin, or he would assume the garb of a prosecuting attorney, get into a wonderful gold-embroidered outfit that belonged to the owner of the summer house he was living in, and deliver an indictment against his friend Levitan—it was a speech which, as his brother attested, "made us all die of laughter". Chekhov brought indictments against Levitan for evading military service, having a secret distillery and maintaining a private pawnshop; he had previously arranged with his friend, the architect Shekhtel, to attend the mock trial in the capacity of judge.

To shove a heavy round watermelon wrapped up in thick paper into the hands of a Moscow policeman and announce to him in a worried yet business-like manner: "Bomb! Take it to the police station—be very careful!" To assure a certain young authoress who was naive to the point of absurdity that his dove with coffee-coloured feathers was a cross between a dove and the cat that lived in his yard —the cat had fur of the same colour. To dress up his brother's wife like a hooligan and provide her with a medical certificate to the effect that she was "suffering from ventriloquism"—he was always up to some prank.

A certain drunken poet fractured his skull. Chekhov went to treat him, and took a young writer along with him. "Who's that with you?" "A young doctor." "Shall I pay him?" "Most certainly." "How much?" "About thirty kopeks."

And the man gratefully handed the young writer thirty kopeks.

In his purely child-like love of fun, practical jokes, buffoonery, masquerading and impromptu theatricals, Chekhov very much resembled that great master of mirth—Dickens.

Once he arrived with the actor Svobodin and a party of other friends in the little town of Akhtyrka, where they put up at the hotel. Svobodin, who was a gifted character actor, pretended to be an important count, and he set the entire hotel aflutter. Chekhov, who played the role of his valet, gave such a convincing performance of the lackey of a pampered count that when people who had been there recalled it forty years later they still could not refrain from laughing.

Another time he was travelling by train with his mother, sister and the 'cellist Semashko. The well-known Moscow Shakespearean scholar, Storozhenko, happened to be in their coach. Chekhov's sister had just left school and regarded her favourite professor with reverent awe. "During the entire trip Masha pretended she did not know me or Semashko," Chekhov recounted in a letter. "In order to punish her for her pettiness I loudly told of the time I had worked as a cook for Countess Keller and spoke of the masters I had had; and before drinking I bowed to my mother every time and expressed the wish that she would find herself a situation (as a servant) in Moscow as quickly as possible. Semashko pretended to be a valet."

Chekhov always got others to take part in these impromptu affairs with him. When he wanted to play the part of a dentist, he had his brother Mikhail put on women's clothes and transform himself into a coquettish maid who admitted the patients—played by several Babkino residents. Until that moment these people undoubtedly had not had the slightest suspicion of their own histrionic ability, but Chekhov so infected them by his gift for improvising that they willingly joined him. When his brother Alexander's turn came, Chekhov shoved an enormous pair of coal-tongs into his mouth and then some real dental "surgery" began. From the very first, Sergeyenko says, all the spectators rocked with laughter. "Then came the climax!

Science was triumphant! Chekhov pulled out of the mouth of the 'patient', who was roaring at the top of his voice, a terrifically large tooth (a cork) and held it up for the public to gaze upon."

III

This is what he was like at that time: tall, graceful, agile, very mobile, with light-brown eyes, and with a magnetic attraction which was felt by everyone.

He never liked to play a solo part in these pranks. His undertakings were always of a gang nature, so to speak.

"We're getting up a game of roulette at our place. . . All the profits go for a common cause: the organization of picnics. I'm the croupier."

"We had a masked ball the other day."

"We're arranging some Olympic games in our yard for the holidays and we're also organizing a game of knucklebones."

He even got old people, despite their weary limbs, to take part in his endless hilarity. Old man Grigorovich was not the same for a long time after he once accidentally dropped in on Chekhov in Moscow during the peak of the excitement which he and his visitors had stirred up there. In the end the old man found himself caught up in a whirlwind of fun. The venerable patriarch, author of *Anton Goremyka* (Anton, the Poor Wretch), later recalled the occasion with mock horror as he raised his hands to heaven:

"If you only knew what went on at the Chekhovs! A bacchanalia! A veritable bacchanalia!"

As often happens among happy, youthful, intimate families, or in regimental or school circles, Chekhov, when speaking to people who were close to him, would employ intimate, amusing nicknames.

Many of these fantastic nicknames stuck to the people for the rest of their lives. Chekhov had an inexhaustible supply of nicknames, and often provided one which was infinitely more suitable than the person's real name.

He dubbed Lika Mizinova—Cantaloup; his brother Nikolai—Squint-Eye; Ivan Shcheglov was the Duke of Alba or Jean or Dear little Jeanne. Seryozha Kiselav, a *gymnasia* pupil, was alternately Grippe or Whooping Cough. Chekhov in his letters referred to himself as Buckle, Count Blackmug, Don Antonio, Academician Toto, or Schiller Shakespearovich Goethe. His brother Alexander called him

Chisel or Thirty-Three Instantly. To Shcheglov he was Antoine and Potemkin, while Yavorsky called him Admiral Avelan.

The same inexhaustible fund of gaiety is also to be found in Chekhov's writings of those days. As he said of himself at the end of the 'eighties, "Vaudeville ideas come gushing out of me like oil out of the bowels of Baku."

The creative energy that constantly seethed in him astonished everyone with whom he came in contact. "Ideas crowded in on him copiously and merrily," Vladimir Korolenko recalls. "His eyes seemed to be an unplumbed ocean of wit and spontaneous mirth."

"Do you know how I write my short stories?" he said to Korolenko just after they had met. "I will tell you. It's like this."

"He glanced at his table," says Korolenko, "took up the first object that met his eye—it happened to be an ash-tray—put it in front of me and said:

" 'If you want it, you'll have a story tomorrow. It will be called *The Ash-Tray.*' "

And it seemed to Korolenko, then and there, that a magical transformation of that ash-tray was taking place: "Certain indefinite situations, adventures which had not yet found concrete form, were already beginning to crystallize about the ash-tray," and were being brought to life through his warm, vital humour.

Everyone marvelled at the mastery and ease with which his powerful fund of creative energy found living form in his host of diverse tales. From his early youth, for a period of ten or twelve years without interruption, Chekhov worked like a dynamo, never stopping for a minute, turning out reams of stuff, and although, at first, not a little of it was scrapped, Chekhov soon began turning out masterpieces by the dozen, one after the other, without pause and without reducing his speed. The writing of every one of these stories displayed a masterly perfection which other talented authors—Vasili Sleptsov, for instance—would have required at least six months to attain. Yet Chekhov dashed them off apparently without the slightest effort, one following on the heels of another, almost daily: *The Order*, and *Surgery*, and *A Grand Mix-Up*, *An Equine Name*, *A Daughter of Albion*, *Murder Will Out*, *A Living Chronology*, *The Chemist's Wife*, *Feminine Happiness*, and countless other stories, every one of which has been an unending source of laughter and delight for half a century and more.

"I read two of Chekhov's books, and laughed like the devil," a peasant once wrote to Maxim Gorky. "I read them to my mother and wife, and they did the same—they simply rolled about with laughter. Now here we've got something that's both funny and beautiful."

That was thirty years ago. But only the other day, in 1944, here in Moscow, some medical students who had to go on night duty borrowed a volume of Chekhov's stories from me. They read and laughed the whole night through until they got hiccoughs. "Our watch was over and it was time to pack up, but we still sat there reading and laughing like silly old fools!"

This humour of Chekhov's has lived through so many world-shaking events—through three wars and three revolutions! How many kingdoms have crumbled, how many famous names have passed into oblivion after having made the world ring with their fame, how many illustrious books have been forgotten, how many changes have taken place in literary trends and styles, yet these "ephemeral" tales of Chekhov's live on in all their freshness, and our grandchildren laugh over them just as heartily as did their fathers and grandfathers. Of course, in Chekhov's own day the critics sneered at these tales with haughty contempt. But what they had regarded as dross turned out to be stainless steel. And indeed every tale proved to have a steel framework so singular, so graceful, so light and yet so enduring, that even legions of imitators who, in the course of half a century, tried to hackney each epithet, each intonation of his, failed to do the slightest harm to these steel-like, indestructible masterpieces.

IV

And then this happiest of talents, this gayest of great Russian writers, a man who infected not only his contemporaries with his immortal mirth but also millions of people yet unborn, suddenly burst forth with an agony of pathos.

Even the young Maxim Gorky, who in those years was by no means inclined to tears—even he gave way before that tempest. Soon after the first publication of Chekhov's story *In the Ravine* in the press, Gorky, who was in Poltava Region, wrote Chekhov:

"I read *In the Ravine* to some muzhiks. If you had only seen the effect it had. Those Khokhols* wept, and I wept with them."

On more than one occasion Gorky remarked on how Chekhov moved him to tears.

"How many wonderful moments your books have given me, and

---

* Khokhols—a good-natured, teasing nickname for Ukrainians.—K.C.

how many times I've wept over them," he wrote in his very first letter to Chekhov.

Several years later he wrote:

"I saw *Uncle Vanya* a few days ago, saw it and broke down like an old woman, although I'm far from being highly strung."

Uncle Vanya was a favourite play of Gorky's and he saw it a number of times. After its thirty-ninth performance he wrote Chekhov from Moscow:

"The audience wept, as did the actors."

Such was the depth of Chekhov's pathos that even professional actors who had rehearsed the play half a hundred times, who had performed it thirty-nine times, and for whom it had become part of their daily routine, even they broke down together with their audience, unable to restrain their tears!

How the people of those days loved to surrender to this pathos of Chekhov's! How wonderful it seemed to them, how ennobling, poetic, lofty! And, I repeat, what is most important is the extraordinary power it had: there is no other literature in the world, not another writer who, without piling up horrors, with the help merely of a quiet, subdued lyricism, could wrest so many tears from his audiences!

In short, he proved to be as great a master of pathos as of humour. In both these departments of emotion he proved to be an equally powerful sovereign over the human heart.

In sorrow and in joy Chekhov retained, to his dying breath, his faculty for being enchanted by the world, a marvellous gift with which great poets are endowed in their youth and which remains with them even in their darkest days.

How many of the wisest of the wise have vainly tried—in Dostoyevsky's words—"to love life more than its meaning"—to love it beyond logic and even in spite of all logic; how persistently have they tried to convince both themselves and others that "even if they don't believe in the order of things, the sticky little leaves that appear in the spring are dear to them"—yet this has usually remained a vain protest, for all the sticky little leaves in all the forests and gardens in the world could not hide from them the excruciating "order of things". But Chekhov never had to exert himself in the slightest to give himself up with "all his vitals and his innards" to the enchantment of life, and this is why his books and letters express so much gratitude to the world for the single fact that this world exists. As Pasternak puts it:

> Adoration overcoming
> I watched, worshipping . . .

"You know, it was so lovely looking through the window at the darkening trees, at the river . . . I could surrender my soul to the devil for the pleasure of taking a peep at the warm, evening sky, at the little stream and the tiny puddles. . . What a luxurious thing nature is ! I could just take her and eat her up !"

And Chekhov would go after her like a gourmet after a truffle. There were no clouds in Russia, no sunsets, footpaths, birches, moonlight nights or moonless nights, no March, August, or January landscapes in which he did not regale himself with insatiable greed, and it is symptomatic that his letters deal much more with Nature than, for instance, do the letters of such generally recognized masters of Nature as Tyutchev, Maikov, Turgenyev, Pisemsky and Fet. For Chekhov, Nature was always an event, and when he spoke of her he, who had such a rich command of words, more often than not found but one epithet for it : wonderful.

"During the day the snow comes softly falling down while at night the moon, a luxuriant, wonderful moon, lights up the whole street. It is magnificent !"

"There is something so wonderful, so touching in Nature, that her poetry and novelty compensate for all the discomforts of life. Every day brings a surprise, each one more delightful than the last. The starlings are already here, the water is murmuring everywhere, and the grass is turning green under the thawing snow."

"The weather here is wonderful, amazing. It is so delightful that I am at a loss for words. . ."

He saw in Nature what a lover finds in his beloved—something new and wonderful every minute of the time, and all his letters which speak of Nature are essentially love-letters.

". . . The weather is marvellous. Everything is in blossom, is alive with song and sparkles with beauty. The garden is quite green already, and even the oaks are astir with life. Billions of creatures are being born every day. . ."

The overpowering spell in which Nature held him is strikingly manifest in all his letters :

". . . The weather is maddeningly, desperately wonderful. What a wretch I am for not knowing how to paint. . ."

". . . The weather is wonderful. The roses and asters are in bloom, the pheasants are whirring overhead and the migrating goldfinches and the thrushes fill the air with sound. It is simply marvellous !"

"Two-thirds of my way lay through a forest. The moon shone and I felt so wonderful, better than I had felt for a long time, exactly as though I were returning from a rendezvous. . ."

"Yes, it's lovely in the village now. It's not only lovely; it's even wonderful."

And how tempestuously indignant he could be with Nature when she proved less wonderful than he wanted her to be!

"Villainous weather. . . The road is as dull as can be, enough to make one kick the bucket. . . The sky is as stupid as a cork. . ."

In fact he was so intimate, so close to Nature that in his letters he either raged at her or was delighted with her to the point of rapture—but he could never feel indifferent towards her.

In general, indifference was alien to him—and herein lay the secret of his power as a great artist. Once, in the early nineties, when in the grip of a spell of indifference—not even indifference but world weariness—he hated himself, as though he were suffering from some loathsome disease. To such an extent did he despise indifference! His main, fundamental, ever-present sensation was a ravenous appetite for life, a curiosity about the tangible, concrete world, about all its manifestations and phenomena. He could easily have said of himself what he makes one of his saddest characters say:

"I was ready to embrace and include within my short life everything accessible to man. I wanted to talk, and to read, and to hammer away somewhere in a big factory, to take the watch on some vessel, to plough. I was drawn to the Nevsky Prospect and to the fields, and to the sea—wherever my fancy beckoned."

This was not fantasy, but genuine emotion, something that was inherent in him all the time.

"I am so tempted by all sorts of things now, as though it were the last meal before a fast," he wrote Suvorin in 1894. "I feel I could eat everything: the steppe, and foreign countries, and a good novel. And some force, as though it were a presentiment, urges me along. . . I want to live, and some force keeps drawing me somewhere. I ought to go to Spain and to Africa."

Later, in 1900, when he was already shackled by his fatal disease, he said to a young writer:

"In your place I would go off to India or the devil knows where; I would take two more university degrees."

How passionately did he object to Tolstoy's morose parable, "Does a man need much land?", which proves that although man dreams of laying hold of limitless expanses, all he needs is the six feet that will be set aside for his grave.

"Why, a corpse needs some six feet and not a living man. Man needs not six feet of land, not a farmstead, but the whole globe, all Nature, where he will have room for the full play of all his qualities and the idiosyncrasies of his free spirit. . ."

For "the sun does not rise twice in one day, nor is life given us twice."

How he ridiculed those writers who remained within the four walls of their homes and observed life from Tuchkov bridge; there they lolled in their furnished room, with the room to the right occupied by some old dame who fried a cutlet on a paraffin stove, and the room to the left by some strumpets who banged on their table with beer-bottles. "And in the end the writer begins to view everything from the viewpoint of furnished rooms and writes only of the old dame and of strumpets and dirty napkins."

Chekhov himself, by the time he was thirty, had already been in Vladivostok and Hong-Kong, in Ceylon and Singapore, in Istambul and in India, and had hardly managed to rest up after his last trip when he was on his way to Vienna, Venice, Milan, Florence, Rome, Naples, Monte Carlo and to Paris.

"Before I had a chance to say 'boo' some invisible force was dragging me off into the mysterious distance."

He had only to stay six months in one spot, and his letters were full of his dreams of a new trip.

"My soul yearns for the boundless skies and limitless horizons."

"How terribly I long for a steamer and the wide open spaces in general."

"I feel that if I don't get a whiff of a deck this year I'll begin to hate my homestead."

And thousands of plans:

"Lev Lvovich Tolstoy* visited me and we've arranged to go to America together."

"I'm still waiting for Kovalevsky; we're going to Africa together."

"I'd like to go to the Princes Islands, and to Istambul and to India again, and to Sakhalin Island."

"I'd gladly move towards the North Pole now, to somewhere on Novaya Zemlya."

With his characteristic, energetic expressiveness he described the delights his rovings afforded him:

"I have sailed more than a thousand versts on the Amur, and have seen a million landscapes. . . Truly, I've seen such riches and have enjoyed so many pleasures that even death does not seem so terrible now."

---

* Son of Leo Nikolayevich Tolstoy.

V

But his attitude towards Nature was not confined to a passive contemplation of its "riches" and "splendours". It was not enough for him to appreciate a landscape aesthetically; he forced Nature to his own unbending will, which sought to create and transform life. He could never permit the soil around him to remain barren, and he laboured so fervently to make the land green that when you looked at him it was impossible not to recall those ardent foresters and gardeners whom he described in his writings. In painting the portrait of the fanatical tree-planter, Astrov, in *Uncle Vanya*, Chekhov drew what was essentially a portrait of himself.

This romantic figure of the creator of forests, poetically in love with his trees, was so dear to Chekhov that he had recourse to this type three times within several years:

First—in a letter to Suvorin, where the sylviculturist appears in the person of the landscape gardener Korovin, who, in his childhood, planted a small birch tree in his yard. When it grew green and swayed in the wind, rustling and throwing a small shadow, Korovin's soul was filled with pride: "He had helped God create a new birch tree, he had done something that added one more tree on earth!"

Secondly—Korovin, now the landowner Mikhail Khrushchev, so loves the woods and is so concerned about saving every tree that his neighbours call him the Wood-Demon. Chekhov even made this protector and friend of the woods the pivot of a play which he called *The Wood-Demon*.

Thirdly—in *Uncle Vanya*, Khrushchev, reincarnated as Dr. Astrov, says in the words of the Wood-Demon: "When my ears catch the murmuring of my young forest, which I planted with my own hands, I feel that if a thousand years from now man is happy, I will have contributed my little share in it."

Chekhov could have said all this about himself, for, as in everything else, he was indefatigably active in rendering the soil fruitful. When still a pupil at the *gymnasia* he planted a little vineyard at his home in Taganrog, and he loved to rest in its shade. When he settled down in desolate and barren Melikhovo, he planted about a thousand cherry trees there and filled the bare forest areas with firs, pines, maples, elms, oaks and other leafy trees—and all Melikhovo grew green.

Several years later he settled on a dry, dusty strip of land in the Crimea. He went to work here just as enthusiastically and planted it with cherry trees and mulberries, with palms, cedars, lilac and gooseberry, and, as he himself admitted, he was blissfully happy: "It's so good, so warm and poetic. It's just one grand delight."

Needless to say, he shared his happiness with others on more than one occasion: he sent his relatives in Taganrog seed so that they might grow at least a garden of sorts about their own home. And he presented trees to his neighbour so that he too might have a garden.

In *The Duel*, when Chekhov wanted to prove that Layevsky's parasitic existence was worthless, the first accusation that he levelled at him was that he "had not planted a single tree and had not grown a single blade of grass" in his own garden.

When he conceived the portrait of a humanitarian who preached the wise gospel that boundless love brings happiness, he put the words into the mouth of a horticulturist who had spent his whole life among flowers, for it seemed to Chekhov that a horticulturist was the man most worthy of propagating such a lofty idea.

The need to plant and sow, to tend and to grow, was never still within him. Time and again he asserted in his letters that gardening was his favourite occupation. "It seems to me," he wrote Menshikov in 1900, "that if it were not for literature, I might become a gardener."

And a year later he wrote to his wife:

"Darling, if I were to give up writing and become a gardener now, it would be a very good thing, for it would give me ten more years of life."

Once—in jest, it is true—he asked a member of the Taganrog town council to get him a job as a gardener in the public park.

And, as though keeping them posted about important events, Chekhov would tell his friends and relatives:

"My hyacinths and tulips are coming up."

"The hemp, castor-oil plant and sunflower have already raised their heads above the ground."

"My roses are blooming marvellously. . ." "My roses are extraordinary."

And when his camellia blossomed in Yalta, he hastened to telegraph his wife about it.

In each little flower, as in every animal, he saw a personality, a character, individual qualities. This is also evident from the fact that certain kinds of flowers were especially dear to him while to others he felt hostile. He was not indifferent to flowers any more than he could be indifferent to people.

"You have 600 dahlia plants," he wrote to Leikin. "Why do you want that cold, uninspiring flower? It has an aristocratic, baronial exterior, but nothing whatever behind it. I feel like knocking off its haughty, dull little head with my cane."

Dearest of all to his heart was the cherry tree in blossom. It is no wonder that the title of his last play which he wrote just before his death was *The Cherry Orchard*—"all white", "young", and "full of happiness".

When he told Stanislavsky that he was going to call his play *The Cherry Orchard*, Chekhov, to Stanislavsky's considerable astonishment, was overcome by sheer joyous laughter, and it struck the latter then that Chekhov was "talking about something wonderful, something he loved tenderly".

Even more wonderful, and more beloved, is the garden depicted by Chekhov in *The Black Monk*, which embodies all the happiness of the great horticulturist Pesotsky.

In both his plays and his stories, when Chekhov desired to depict a catastrophe in the life of people, he presented it in the terms of the desolation of their beloved garden. For the horticulturist Pesotsky, the desolation of his garden and death were one and the same thing.

VI

Not only was Chekhov eager to turn everything green, to make the soil fruitful; he was also always eager to create something new in life.

With all his positive, dynamic, inexhaustibly active nature that said "yes" to life so emphatically, he gave himself up not merely to describing life, but to transforming it, to reconstructing it.

Now he would bustle about the building of Moscow's first People's Home, with a library, reading-room, auditorium and theatre.

Now he would see about getting Moscow a clinic for skin diseases.

Now with the help of Ilya Repin he would organize a Museum of Painting and Fine Arts in Taganrog.

Now he would initiate the building of the Crimea's first biological station.

Now he would collect books for all of Sakhalin's schools and ship them there in large consignments.

Now he would build three schools for peasant children not far from Moscow, one after the other, and, at the same time, a belfry and a fire station for the peasants.

Later, when he moved to the Crimea, he built a fourth school there.

In general, any constructional work fascinated him, for in his opinion construction always increased the sum total of man's happiness.

"I remember his childlike joy," Stanislavsky says, "when I once told him about a huge house that was going up at Krasnye Vorota on the site of a wretched, one-storey building that had been pulled down. For a long time afterwards Anton Pavlovich talked enthusiastically about this to everyone who came to see him !"

Once Gorky read him his proud hymn, man the builder, who thirsted to transform the entire planet by constantly tilling the soil and building. The hymn contained these lines:

> I'd roam the world and plough it all over,
> I'd roam for centuries building city after city,
> Churches, and gardens without number.
> I'd adorn the earth as if it were a maiden.

This could not fail to please Chekhov, for it fully expressed his own faith in the salutary benefits of our thousand-year-old horticulture and architecture.

"If every man did what he could on his little bit of soil, how marvellous our world would be !" he wrote to Gorky at that time. And in his notebook he made this entry: "The Mussulman digs a well for the salvation of his soul. It would be good if each of us left after him a school, a well or something of the kind, so that our life would not pass into eternity without leaving any trace behind."

It may not be generally known that Chekhov himself put up a monument to Peter I in Taganrog, on Primorsky Boulevard. While he was in Paris he persuaded Antokolsky to sacrifice the statue he had modelled. He arranged to have it cast and delivered free of charge from the port of Marseilles to Taganrog, where he selected the finest site available. His delight in anticipation of this new embellishment to the city was boundless.

"We couldn't have got a finer monument if we'd held a world competition. . . Near the sea it will be picturesque, imposing, and majestic, to say nothing of the fact that the statue portrays the real Peter, Peter the Great, the man of genius, the man of great ideas and great strength."

This constructive fervour of Chekhov's often entailed much hard work for him; when he was building the schools, he himself had all the fuss and bother of dealing with the bricklayers, plumbers and carpenters; he bought all the building materials himself, down to the tiles and doors for the Dutch ovens, and he personally supervised construction work. Almost any one of his letters written during this period gives the impression that it was written by a professional architect or building engineer, so taken up was Chekhov with beams and pilasters, cement and lime and foundations. The buildings proved to be model ones: "with Dutch ovens, and a large apartment with a fireplace for each teacher". Conscientiously Chekhov looked on it as his duty to devote all his energy to this job, just as he did with anything else he undertook.

And when he conceived his plan of building a public library in his native Taganrog, on such a large scale as provincial towns never even dreamed of having in those days, he not only gave up more than two thousand of his own books, that is, his entire personal library which contained many rare autographed editions of considerable value, he not only set up a picture gallery for the library, with portraits of outstanding scientists and artists, but for the next fourteeen years he kept sending it bundles and cases of books he purchased. Such consistent generosity was typical.

When he was in Nice—towards the end of the 'nineties—he wrote:

"To open a foreign department in the library I've bought all the French classics and have just sent them on to Taganrog. Altogether 70 authors, 319 volumes."

All the French classics. Three hundred and nineteen volumes. And this at a time when he was running short of money.

Take his work as a district doctor. During a cholera epidemic he looked after twenty-five villages absolutely singlehanded. And the help he gave to the starving during the years when the harvest failed. And his work during the All-Russian census. And his many years of medical practice as a doctor, chiefly among the peasants of Moscow's suburbs.

According to his sister, Maria Pavlovna, who helped him as a trained nurse, he "treated more than a thousand sick peasants a year at his home, gratis, besides which he supplied them all with medicines".

But what I wish to emphasize here is not his generosity so much as his colossal energy, his passionate striving to take such an active part in life in order that people might live more wisely and more happily.

In 1889, when he was planning to purchase, on credit, a "mangy little homestead" on the Khorol River, he wrote to Pleshcheyev, who was in St. Petersburg:

"If I do succeed in buying something, I'll add on a few wings and lay the foundation for a literary colony on the banks of the Khorol."

He did not found this colony, any more than he erected the lodging-house which he had long dreamed of building, or the sanatorium for ailing teachers, with a fruit orchard, kitchen garden and apiary attached, which Gorky mentions in his reminiscences. But what he did do was more than enough. When he died he left behind not only twenty volumes of universally famous prose, but also four village schools, a highroad to Lopasnya, a library for an entire city, a monument to Peter I, a belfry, a forest which he had planted on waste land and two wonderful gardens.

VII

And a pile of letters from hundreds and hundreds of grateful people.

Over seven thousand letters addressed to Chekhov have been preserved. The Socio-Economic Publishing House recently published excerpts from this mountain of mail and everywhere we meet that rarest of words: Gratitude.

"I am most grateful for the money received."

"I am most grateful to you for helping me find work."

"I am so grateful to you for bothering about the passport."

"I am deeply grateful for the financial assistance."

And there are numerous publishers' comments such as the following:

"The undersigned enjoyed Chekhov's support . . ." "Chekhov helped the son of the undersigned . . ." "Chekhov lent Kirin money for a trip to Kolomna".

Nor could it have been otherwise. All Chekhov's relations with people were like that: he took very little from them, usually nothing at all, but he gave unstintingly and kept no record.

What a fund of energy he must have possessed to have enough for everyone—literally everyone who appealed to him for help of any kind.

If I were to enumerate all the poems, novels, novelettes and short stories written by the Belousovs, Kruglovs, Mendeleviches, Gurlyands, Kiselevs, Likhachevs, Ostrovskys, Lazarevskys and Petrovs which Chekhov helped them to get printed, one might think I was writing not of one person who was head over heels engaged in his own work, but of some large, well-organized literary agency employing a staff of energetic people and possessing an excellently organized literary consultation bureau.

A young writer named Shavrova sent Chekhov not two or three of her stories but nine—nine stories, one after another! He spent a great deal of time on each one, corrected them, sent them to various publishing houses and finally addressed her with the request:

"Write twenty more stories and send them along. I'll read them through with pleasure."

And inasmuch as "creative work gushed forth from him like oil from the bowels of Baku", he by no means confined himself to a passive appraisal of the manuscript, but with his usual energy he plunged into the work of the author who had appealed to him for advice, and generously gave her of his own rich experience and fantasy.

Once someone sent him a short story called *The Singer*.

"I've made the middle of *The Singer* the beginning, and the beginning the middle, and I've given it quite a new ending."

The creative energy which he spent on others was staggering.

VIII

With the same extraordinary generosity he arranged for the staging of the plays of others.

At the end of the 'eighties, when he had just got to know the actors of the Maly and the Korsh Theatres, he began sending out to playwrights of his acquaintance the following letters, which could almost be called circulars:

"Should you write a play during the summer, wouldn't you like to have it put on at the Maly Theatre in Moscow? If you should, I'm at your command."

And another:

"Hasn't Maslov any play on hand? I'd like it to be put on at the Korsh."

He didn't wait for Maslov to ask him to take up the production of his play with the Korsh Theatre. He did not even know if Maslov had written a play. But he hazarded a guess at Maslov's wishes and proffered his friendly help which the other had not even thought of asking.

A third letter:

"You're writing a play? Finish it and authorize me to put it on for you in Moscow. I'll attend the rehearsals, collect your royalties for you and do any other little thing. . ."

And when Suvorin, who had written *Repina*, actually did authorize him to have it put on in Moscow, Chekhov exerted much more effort and fussed a great deal more about it than he did about the production of his own plays. He surmounted all the petty squabbles that went on behind the scenes, and overcame the stubbornness of the conceited actors, and this production, under Chekhov's direction, proved to be incomparably more painstaking than the one which the author of the play himself supervised in St. Petersburg.

Several years later, when his own plays began appearing at the Moscow Art Theatre, Chekhov, true to his everlasting custom, drew other writers to this theatre. The Russian drama is largely indebted to Chekhov for the fact that Gorky wrote *The Philistines* and *The Lower Depths* for the Art Theatre.

"I'm urging all the finest authors to write for the Art Theatre," Chekhov told his wife in 1901. "Gorky has already done so. Balmont, Leonid Andreyev, Teleshov and others are doing so now. I think I deserve at least a ruble for each author."

IX

"We must help all who ask, without exception, and not be afraid of being deceived. It is better to be deceived than to deceive oneself."

Sakhalin Island, Ch. XVII.

But all this had to do with literature, whereas Chekhov is remarkable in that he was ready to serve, in all their everyday affairs, those both close to him or distant.

"Should there be anything you would like me to do, don't stand on ceremony but tell me what it is; I am at your service," he wrote Lintvareva, for instance.

And she was only one of dozens.

"If you want me to, I'll have a look at the estate you're being offered."

"Isn't there anything I can buy for you in the way of fishing tackle?"

"Time would pass," Sergei Shchukin recalls; "you yourself would already have forgotten what you had asked him to do, and suddenly he would let you know that at last he had done what you wanted, and there he was with the answer to your request: you would be surprised, then you would remember what it was all about, and be so ashamed that you had made him trouble himself about it."

Immediately after performing some difficult service for Suvorin, Chekhov asked him not to hesitate if there was anything else he wanted:

"If it's necessary to go to hell, I'll do it. Only please don't stand on ceremony with me."

And he even thanked those friends who came running to him with their difficulties:

"Thanks for not standing on ceremony and for appealing to me," he wrote Savelyev in 1884. "Don't think you're putting me out at all. . . Please don't stand on ceremony and, most important, don't hesitate. . ."

And they did not hesitate. No one did. He helped them until he went to the grave. What is so remarkable about him is that he was so glad at any opportunity to bring joy to other people that he did not even make any attempt to discriminate between them, to decide whether they were worthy of his help or whether he, Chekhov, wanted to do the thing they asked him to do.

He himself had an aversion for the orders and ranks of the day, but when a certain ambitious old man told him that it was his sacred dream to get a Bulgarian order for his participation in the Russo-Turkish War, Chekhov took great pleasure in getting the order for the old fellow.

It is hardly likely that Chekhov had much interest in the intentions of a certain young man to marry his own cousin—he had never set eyes on either of them. But he took a most active part in arranging this wedding, just as he did in arranging many others. He even asked lawyers how best to avoid the law forbidding the marriage of relatives, and corresponded with a priest on the matter.

Nor was it by any means necessary for him to like those who came to him with a request of one sort or another. In 1891 he tried to prevent a certain Martha Ivanovna's discharge from work—she was a saleswoman at a bookstall in one of the Ukrainian railway stations —although from his letter it was evident how much he disliked this cantankerous scandalmonger.

He was firmly convinced that not only those people had a right to our help whose interests were the same as ours or who were close to our hearts but also those like that "Mugface" who brought him her manuscript and sat with him for an hour and a half, upsetting him as well as his plans for work, and concerning whom he wrote:

"Send her some consoling word, some hope for the future. . ."

"Don't crush her with a cold cruel reply. Soften it down a bit somehow. . ." "Mugface is awful."

At the end of 1903, when he had but a few months left to live, when a single glance at him was enough to show how hard it was for him to move, how difficult for him to breathe—at that time a Yalta resident, Barbara Kharkeyevich, asked him to take her watch along with him to Moscow to have it repaired. When Chekhov reached Moscow, he took the watch to a watchmaker's on Kuznetsky Most. The man tested it for two weeks, and at the end of that time told Chekhov, when he came back for it, that the watch was no good. Chekhov wrote to Barbara Kharkeyevich and, of course, added that if she wished him to do so he would gladly try to sell the watch for her and buy her a new one. She readily agreed. And he, although deathly ill, again set off to a watchmaker's, sold her watch and bought her a new one. In his letter to her he wrote ;

"The watch is an excellent one. I bought it with a hundred-year guarantee from the best watchmaker, Bouret, and bargained long and successfully with the shopkeeper."

Needless to say, Chekhov did not as a rule waste his energy on such trivial matters, but concerned himself primarily with all sorts of people who were really in need.

A whole book could be written about his work in Yalta as a member of the Board of Guardians for the "Visiting Sick". Chekhov burdened himself to such an extent that he was practically the entire institution in himself, the entire Board of Guardians. Many tubercular people came to Yalta at that time, without a copper in their pocket; they came all the way from Odessa, Kishinov and Kharkov just because they had heard that Chekhov was living in Yalta. "Chekhov will fix us up, Chekhov will arrange board and lodging for us and treatment."

And they besieged him the whole day long. He complained that it was excruciatingly difficult—he himself was wasting away with the disease—yet every day he went about fixing them up, and if they were Jews he secured for them the right to live in Yalta.

He was almost unable to get rid of the spongers whom, as soon as they learned he had arranged for the publication of a complete collection of his works, came flying down on him like a swarm of locusts. He had little money at the time. His publisher, a cunning old fox, cheated him most unscrupulously; yet there were moments when he had a little money left, and this he distributed to scores of people.

"I spend an incredible amount of money daily, an incredible amount," he wrote Olga Knipper at the time. "Yesterday someone got a hundred rubles out of me, today someone else came to say good-bye and I gave him ten rubles, someone else—a hundred rubles. I promised another a hundred rubles, and still another fifty rubles, and I've got to let them all have it tomorrow."

Chekhov would become angry with himself at his own liberality, but if possible he never refused anyone anything, for one of his time-honoured foibles was to "lend without repayment". And he did this secretly, so that even those who were close to him, like the actor Vishnevsky of the Art Theatre, considered him "somewhat stingy".

"I haven't a dressing-gown," he wrote his wife. "I let someone have mine but I don't remember who it was."

On June 2, 1904, when he was literally on his deathbed, he tried to arrange for the transfer of a student, the son of a deacon, from one university to another.

"I've already sent a certain gentleman today to see the rector about it," he wrote to the deacon, "and tomorrow I'll talk to some-one else. I'll be back at the end of July or the beginning of August, and then I'll do everything I can to satisfy your desire—with which I am wholly in sympathy."

This, it appears, was the first time a person appealed to Chekhov for help and did not receive what he wanted. And for a perfectly plausible reason: exactly one month later Chekhov died—died before the date he had designated in his letter.

All other requests he satisfied, although it remains impossible to understand how he found the time.

This was not philanthropy of the kind that lulls the conscience of the givers who, by means of sops, large or small, distract the "have-nots" from battling against an unjust order.

Chekhov was of a different stamp: he was the author of *Sakhalin Island, The Man in the Muffler, Ionych, My Life, Ward No. 6* and *Mouzhiks*, works which constituted a fierce indictment of all the inhumanity of those days. His daily, active compassion for indi-vidual, miserable, human creatures was always combined with his struggle for the happiness of the oppressed masses, and only dolts, those whom Herzen called the "dull of heart", can call Chekhov a "typical philanthropist".

For some reason or other these "dull-hearted people" decided that their participation—at times highly abstract in form—in a collec-tive effort against a social lie completely absolves them of any concern for each separate needy individual. And as it is much easier to love mankind as a whole than to love individuals, they have denounced individual help to definite people as niggardly, reactionary charity. Chekhov, however, never forgot that love for mankind is effective only when it is supplemented by active sympathy for the fates of individual human beings. Compassion for the concrete individual was his cult. Even simple people who had never read Chekhov felt he was someone who "suffered" with them. Kuprin relates that when, on board a steamer in the port of Yalta, a certain Prishibeyev struck one of the porters in the face in Chekhov's presence, the porter cried out at the top of his voice:

"What? You hit me? Do you think it's me you hit? You swine, that's the man you hit!"

And he pointed to Chekhov. Even he understood that for Chekhov another man's pain was also his own.

X

Greatly as I admire Chekhov's wonderful attitude towards people, it is not so much his outstanding tenderness and affection that I wish to stress as the inexhaustibility of his vitality, which was felt in everything he did. We have just seen that:

As a writer he worked like a dynamo.

He helped people energetically and tirelessly as though he were not one man but an entire institution.

He even received visitors in such unheard-of numbers that his home might have been taken for a hotel. . .

Thus, the first thing to be said of him is that he was a man of phenomenal energy, with an extraordinary fund of spiritual and emotional power. What seems totally incomprehensible is why no one has noted this most important feature in Chekhov before.

His participation in the creation of things, the schools he built, his gardens, libraries and buildings to which he devoted all his leisure time, are concrete evidence of the superabundance of his constructive energy.

And when I say that, even in his early years, his avidly keen glance seized on impressions and images that normally would require a thousand pairs of eyes, it is not mere rhetoric but the objective truth. If we compare, for instance, the range of observation of his most talented predecessors, such masters of the short story as Vasily Sleptsov and Nikolai Uspensky, the colossal diversity of the impressions and sensations which Chekhov accumulated by the time he was twenty-five seems almost superhuman.

He was equally outstanding as a humorist. The greatest Russian humorist after Gogol, he infected not only his contemporaries with his Chekhovian laughter but also millions of their grandchildren and great-grandchildren.

I will not dwell on the fact that he shouldered the burden of the entire literature of the 'eighties. Not without reason was his period called the Chekhov period; he was its central figure. He towers alone over it like a Colossus, for although he remained at loggerheads with all its trends and was its perpetual opponent, yet he was also its most powerful exponent.

The question naturally arises: Why was it that to the end of his days no one realized his true giant stature? Even those who loved him constantly referred to him as "dear Chekhov", "lovable Chekhov", "exquisite Chekhov", "refined Chekhov", "pathetic Chekhov", "charming Chekhov", as though they were referring not to a man of immense proportions but to a figurine that was attractive exactly because of its delicate diminutiveness.

Not only during his lifetime but also afterwards, right up to the present, even those who loved him seem to think that the words "enormous" and "mighty" are quite incongruous when applied to him. But the main question is: Why did he himself, in the face of all evidence to the contrary, stubbornly reject these appellations?

CHAPTER TWO

". . . I've purposely set myself a task beyond my strength. . ."
". . . I'm being my own 'animal-trainer' at every opportunity."

From *Anton Chekhov's Letters.*

"With whom did he wage the ceaseless struggle?
With him himself, with him himself."

BORIS PASTERNAK.

I

THERE WAS A SEVERE AND CAPTIOUS CRITIC IN RUSSIA WHO WAS STUB-bornly hostile to Chekhov's brilliant work and who, over a long period of years, heaped scorn on his head as an inferior scribbler.

Even today, after a lapse of half a century, it hurts to read his malicious, insolent comments on the works of the great writer. "Junk", "rubbish", "trash", "a chewed rag", "colophony and vinegar", "ponderous twaddle", "not art but muck"—such were the usual epithets which this critic applied to almost every new production of Chekhov's.

Chekhov's play *Ivanov* had not as yet appeared in print when this critic called it "*bolvanov*" (chucklehead), "a miscarriage", "a nasty little skit". Even his wonderful story *The Steppe*, which is the only lyrical hymn to the limitless expanses of Russia to be found anywhere in world literature, was, in this critic's opinion, "a bagatelle", while Chekhov's earlier *chefs-d'œuvre*, such as *The Malefactor*, *The Eve of the Trial, First Aid, A Work of Art*, masterpieces which have now become an inherent part of world literature, were declared, in the same contemptuous tone, to be "bad and banal". . . . *A Tragedian in Spite of Himself* was considered a "mangy piece", an "old, stale joke", and *The Proposal*, a "notoriously stupid little play" . . .

What is most remarkable is the fact that this heartless and cavilling critic, who so angrily condemned almost every work of Chekhov's, was—Chekhov himself. It was he who called his plays "trifling skits", and his tales—"rubbish and junk".

About two thousand letters of his, written to his relatives, friends and acquaintances, have come down to us, and it is characteristic of him that in not a single one of them does he refer to his creative art as such. He seems to have fought shy of applying such a high-sounding, lofty term to his own literary work. When a certain authoress called him a proud master, he hurriedly and jestingly disclaimed all right to that imposing title.

"Why call me a proud master? Only turkeys are proud."

He felt he did not have the right to call his inspired writing "creative art", and in all his letters, especially those written during the first decade of his career, he speaks of it in a deliberately scornful tone:

"I've scratched off a mangy little vaudeville sketch, a banal, dullish little thing. . ." "I'll try to scratch off a sour little trifle. . ." "Your letter reached me as I was scratching off a wretched little story. . ." "I've spun off a tale. . ." "Somehow or other I've got off two stories. . ." "In between things I've dashed off a comedy. . ."

"Dashed off", "got off", "spun off", "scratched off"—these are the only terms in which he spoke of the mighty, complex processes of his creative art, no matter whether he was referring to *A Dull Story* or *The Duel* or *Vanka*, which today are included in all anthologies, or to *The Birthday*, executed with truly Tolstoyan force.

Although later he gave up using such expressions, he continued this harsh condemnation of his finest compositions:

"I've just finished a play, which I'm calling *The Sea-gull*. Nothing especially good. Generally speaking, I'm no great shakes as a playwright."

"A monstrously dull thing," he wrote of his story *Fires*. "And it contains so much philosophizing that it's cloying. . ." "I'm re-reading what I've written and I'm slobbering with disgust, it's so nauseating. . ."

Although by the end of the 'eighties, Chekhov had come to occupy first place among the writers of his generation, he continued in his letters to declare that if writers were listed according to their importance, he would be thirty-seventh among Russian writers of fiction. Even this, however, must have sounded like bragging to him, for soon after, in a letter to a relative in Taganrog, he substituted a still more modest figure. Referring to Chaikovsky, Chekhov wrote: "He is now celebrity No. 2 in St. Petersburg and Moscow; Leo Tolstoy is considered No. 1, whereas I am No. 877."

It was as if, in his youth, he had solemnly made a vow never to brag of his literary achievements to anyone and never to reveal to anyone how earnest, severe and exacting he was in respect to his own gifts. Himself one of the profoundest of writers, he often speaks of his levity. "Of the Russians writing today, I am the most light-minded and least serious," he said in a letter written in 1887 to Vladimir Korolenko after he had written such stirring things as *Happiness*, *Home*, *Verochka*, *A Bad Business*, and that very significant story, *En Route*, which, in Korolenko's opinion, showed an astonishingly true understanding of the very essence of those "Russian seekers for something nobler" who were wandering all over the face of the earth.

True to his custom, Chekhov concealed from others the difficult aspects of his work, and nothing in the world would induce him to let anyone know what great efforts his creative art demanded of him. He applied himself to his writing with superhuman energy, but even to his closest friends he very rarely spoke of how difficult it was for him to write.

Such admissions as these are unusual for him:

"I've written a story . . . fussed over it for whole days and nights on end, sweated a lot over it, and feel I've almost grown silly with the exertion. . . I've got writer's cramp and the devil only knows what nightmares I've had."

On the contrary, on every possible occasion Chekhov speaks of his apparently supernatural laziness: "I'm idling wonderfully. . ." "Astonishing indolence. . ." "I'm the laziest of all fiction writers . . ." "The lazy Khokhol blood runs in my veins. . ." "I'm idling as usual. . ." "I'm spending the days doing nothing. . ." "I'm a Khokhol—I'm lazy." "Idleness agreeably intoxicates me, like

c

ether. . ." "The Khokhol laziness is getting the upper hand over my other feelings. . ."

He did not want others to divine the tremendous amount of work he performed, work that taxed his strength; and so in his letters he always pictured his rare moments of rest as though they were his usual condition.

When he was awarded the Pushkin Prize by the Academy of Sciences in 1888 for his *Stories*, he wrote in one of his letters:

"It must have been for the crab-catches I made."

Much of this, no doubt, is to be explained by his unparalleled reticence, his unwillingness to introduce outsiders to his emotional life.

"There are no people around me who have need of my confidence or who have the right to it," he admitted in one of his frankest letters. He had long formed the habit of concealing from most of the people about him everything concerning his creative self; he preferred to evade the issue with a joke rather than lift the veil from his inner world. The perfunctory, ironical manner in which he referred to his own writing often served him as a protection against unwonted curiosity and interference on the part of others.

But more often than not it was a case of "divine discontent" with himself, a quality which, it seems, is especially characteristic of Russian talent.

Chekhov manifested this dissatisfaction with himself most strikingly in 1887–89, when he first became famous.

II

Fame came to Chekhov most unexpectedly. Only a short time before he had been lost in the vulgar crowd of third-rate scribblers in the second-rate press, lost among all the possible Popudoglos, Bilibins, Lazarevs, Gilyarovskys, "Emile Poops", Kicheyevs and other literary pygmies. Gradually, however, admiration for his talent began to spread in St. Petersburg, at first among individuals and later among whole phalanxes of connoisseurs and critics, who grew louder and louder in their praise of him until, when he finally made a trip to St. Petersburg, he met, to his amazement, with such an enthusiastic reception that his head, as he later admitted, "felt dizzy for about two months from those laudatory fumes".

"I returned from St. Petersburg a few days ago. I bathed in glory there and sniffed the aromatic scent of the gods."

"I am the most fashionable writer in St. Petersburg," he said in letters to his relatives.

This "sniffing the scent of the gods" promised him a stable future and, first and foremost, freedom from the exhausting poverty which had oppressed him ever since childhood. When a student he had had to support his sister, brother, mother and father; now, after a whole decade of strenuous work, he found he could breathe freely for the first time.

Furthermore, his sudden fame introduced him to a select circle of the most outstanding Russians, personages of whom his colleagues on the comic weeklies *The Cricket* and *The Alarm-Clock* could only dream. It was no longer Kicheyev and Lazarev who accepted him into their midst, but Korolenko, Grigorovich, Terpigorev, Maximov, Leskov, Fofanov, Polonsky, Pleshcheyev, and the great Chaikovsky.

Immediately upon reading *The Steppe* in manuscript form, Pleshcheyev wrote Chekhov:

"It is so charming and embraces such a world of poetry that the only thing I can tell you, the only comment I can make, is that I am in wild ecstasy over it. . . It's a long time since I have read anything with such tremendous enjoyment. . . Garshin is crazy about it. . . Boborykin is madly enthusiastic about you and considers you the most gifted of all living fiction writers."

"Your most sincere admirer," is how Chaikovsky ended a letter he sent him.

"To Anton Pavlovich Chekhov, from an admirer of his talent," Polonsky inscribed in a copy of his book which he presented to Chekhov.

There was only one young writer whom certain magazine critics placed on a level with Chekhov, but Grigorovich indignantly protested against the comparison:

"Why, he's not fit to kiss the foot of a flea that bites Chekhov!"

It was during this happy period that Chekhov's talent blossomed forth and developed to the most remarkable extent. After his play *Ivanov*, which was so successful on the stage of the Alexandrinsky Theatre, focussing attention on the most burning questions of the day, and his tale *The Fit*, which was a profound study of the painful Garshin theme of our personal guilt in relation to the victims of the social order, Chekhov published *A Dull Story*, and even Mikhailovsky, who had been hostile to him and had revealed a total inability to understand Chekhov's art, came out with a critical review in which he stated that it was "the best and most significant thing" Chekhov had yet written.

Concerning the first edition of his volume of *Short Stories*, Pleshcheyev wrote him from St. Petersburg:

"I hear your book is selling wonderfully and new editions cannot be put out quickly enough."

He was so successful that he was enviously dubbed "Potemkin". "Fortune's lone pet" is what he said of himself.

In 1889 an exhibition of Semiradsky's paintings was opened with great pomp in the capital, and among them one that was especially successful was a nude of the beautiful Phryne, surrounded by an enraptured crowd.

"There are two heroes of the day in St. Petersburg now," Chekhov wrote; "Semiradsky's naked Phryne, and myself fully dressed."

But the more his work was extolled and the more ardently his admirers praised him (one even proclaimed him to be the elephant of all fiction writers), the more remorseless was he in his attitude towards himself and his work. In a letter written at the end of 1889, summing up his literary achievements during this period, which was the happiest of his entire career as a writer, Chekhov stated: Behind me there is "a mountain of mistakes, tons of paper covered with writing, an Academy prize and the life of a Potemkin, yet in spite of all this there is not a single line which, in my opinion, possesses real literary value. I so very much want to hide somewhere for about five years and do a piece of painstaking, serious work. I must study, learn everything from the very beginning, for as a writer I'm an all-round ignoramus."*

He was even harsher in another letter:

"My work is so paltry that I don't derive any satisfaction from it. . . It is never too early to ask oneself: am I doing something real or is it all worthless? . . . I have a feeling I'm just writing trash."

In other letters he repeats the same thing:

"No, we're not writing what's necessary."

"There are moments when the spirit positively quails. For whom, for what, am I writing? For the public? I can't decide whether the public needs me or not."

"I'm sick to the point of nausea with reading Chekhov."

"I don't like the idea that I'm successful. What hurts is that the gibberish has already been written, while what's good is lying about in my mental warehouse like so much lumber. . ."

Thus, in the midst of his most brilliant literary success, this "pet of fortune" expressed his painful dissatisfaction not with one or another of his works, but with all his writing, with its entire meaning.

---

* The beginning of this letter has not been preserved and the first four words are, therefore, hypothetical.

Just when he was basking in the rays of his growing fame he wanted to hide, to go off somewhere where it was quiet, into obscurity, so that after working five years or so over some difficult job he might do something real at last, something urgently necessary to man, for, as he put it at that time, "modern fiction is absolutely unnecessary". And in another place he explained that even at its best it merely "helps the devil multiply snails and woodlice".

Fiction, the only cause to which up to that time he had devoted his whole being, the artistic representation of contemporary Russian reality, seemed to him to be "flippant, unnecessary" and "nonsense".

And so he decided to put an end to this "nonsense".

"I feel drawn to work, but not literary work. I am fed up with that. . ."

This refusal to serve art, this repudiation by an artist of his own mastery, is quite characteristic of men of great talent. The world over you will find few people with such titanic powers as Gogol and Leo Tolstoy, who, at the very height of their glory, suddenly began to scorn the great things they had created and, regarding their art as unnecessary, forced themselves to abandon it for what seemed to them more useful service to humanity.

The same thing, although fortunately not for long, happened to Chekhov. But whereas Gogol and Tolstoy voiced their renunciation of creative art demonstratively and loudly so that it resounded throughout Russia, throughout the world, Chekhov, true to his Chekhovian reticence, left the world of fiction in silence, without declarations or sermons, so that even his biographers were unaware of it.

Chekhov's bitter thoughts about the futility of his stories were not the expression of the typical artist's fleeting disenchantment with and lack of confidence in his work. His was a deep-seated feeling. Otherwise it could not have prompted him to commit what his contemporaries described as the "act of a madman", or, as we say now, an act of self-sacrifice. The act was a rash, needless one, but for all that it was an act. I am referring to Chekhov's journey to Sakhalin Island to study the life of those sentenced to terms of penal servitude there.

III

Most authors who have written about Chekhov have remarked on their utter inability to understand whatever induced him, in

1890, to undertake so dangerous and fatiguing a trip without any apparent reason for it.

"I still don't understand Chekhov's journey to Sakhalin," Yezhov declares. "Why did he go there? Perhaps to find plots. I don't know."

"The reasons prompting Chekhov to make that exceptionally difficult journey have to this day remained inadequately explained," writes Sergei Balukhaty.

Yet one only needs to recall Chekhov's deep dissatisfaction with himself, which particularly obsessed him at that time, dissatisfaction with his own art and achievements, for his act to become fully comprehensible. Precisely because the whole business was so difficult, tiring and dangerous, precisely because it took him away from the happy career of a successful, fashionable author, he burdened himself with this undertaking.

As his sister Maria Pavlovna later stated, "at that time there were rumours of the difficult conditions of exiles condemned to penal servitude on Sakhalin Island. People were indignant, they grumbled about it, but that was all, no one took any measures. . . Anton Pavlovich, however, could not remain calm when he knew that people were suffering in exile. He decided to go out there."

He had never spared himself, nor did he display the slightest self-indulgence on this occasion. Other writers, as soon as they acquired fame and were no longer hard up, travelled abroad, to Paris, to Rome. But Chekhov sentenced himself to a convict island. At that time he had not yet been abroad and he was very much tempted to go. Toward the end of the 'eighties—not long before he went to Sakhalin—he had made dozens of plans for a pleasure trip through Europe:

"I'd like to live on the Luka until June, and then take a trip to Paris, to the French girls. . ."

"We're all fools for not going to the exhibition in Paris. We'll die without having seen anything. . ."

"I'm going to St. Petersburg to caution off my novel. Then I'll leave for the Pyrenees."

"What a pleasure it would be to go off somewhere, to Biarritz, where the orchestra plays and there are plenty of women. . ."

He could have rested on the shore of the Mediterranean, but he forced himself, sick man though he was, to set off for the most pernicious spot to be found in all Russia. And in doing so, he explained laconically:

"I must be my own animal-trainer!"

"The journey means a good six months of uninterrupted physical

and mental labour," he wrote in one of his letters, "but I must do it
for I'm a Khokhol and have begun to feel lazy; I must train
myself."

He spent a long time preparing for his Sakhalin trip, and studied
a whole library of scientific volumes as well as all manner of news-
papers and magazines which had even the remotest connection with
the devils' island he was preparing to visit. He studied the geology of
Sakhalin, its flora and fauna, its history and ethnography; at the same
time he made a detailed study of prison administration, inasmuch as
he wished to challenge the Russian system of penal servitude, not in the
capacity of a light-weight pamphleteer, but as a serious, well-equipped
scientist.

It was in this way that he divorced himself from fiction, which had
become repellent to him. Fiction had brought him fame and money,
but—"I must be my own animal-trainer", and so, for whole months
at a time, he stayed indoors and studied "the soil, the subsoil, sandy
loam, and loamy sand".

"Such a tedious, cursed job, it seems I'll die with boredom. . .
Cockroaches are roosting in my brain. . ."

No sooner did he finish this tedious job than he immediately set
off for the place to which people were usually driven by force, across
the whole of Siberia, thousands and thousands of miles, travelling
by horse—there were no railways there at that time, in a sort of gig
during the bad season when roads were full of bumps, ruts and holes,
"the only ones in the world" which shook a person's soul out of him,
and repeatedly broke the wheels and axles of his cart. He was so
cruelly jolted by the journey, especially beyond Tomsk, that all his
joints ached severely. His valises would go flying out of the gig into
the ruts. His hands and feet were numb with cold, and he had
scarcely anything to eat, for in his inexperience he had neglected to
take along the necessary food supply. On more than one occasion he
nearly lost his life: one night he was thrown out into the road, and
two other carts, each hauled by a team of three horses, nearly lumbered
over him. Another time the steamer in which he was going down
one of the Siberian rivers struck some submerged rocks.

It was not these dangers, however, that mattered, so much as the
countless deprivations and suffering which Chekhov had to endure
en route. It is painful to read his letters in which he tells how, while
ploughing ahead in a cart, despite the spring floods he had to keep
jumping out in his felt boots into the cold water in order to hold the
horses. "I'm swimming across a river; it's raining cats and dogs,
the wind's howling, the baggage is getting soaked and my felt boots
are a cold, clinging, soggy mess." Added to all this, he had many a

sleepless night, for it was impossible to stretch out in his uncomfortable vehicle.

Yet he kept forging doggedly ahead, and he would not have been Chekhov if, after all these torments, he had not written to one of his acquaintances from some station *en route*:

"Quite a good journey. . ."

Here again we see his usual reluctance to make a fuss about himself and his actions. Yet this Sakhalin trip was a very definite action. There had been Russian writers before him who had made a study of convict life, but in almost every case this had been brought about involuntarily: Dostoyevsky, Korolenko and Melshin have left us remarkable books about life in penal servitude; each of them served terms of exile. But for a young writer, in the heyday of his career, to set off voluntarily over a murderous route of over six thousand miles where there were no roads fit for travel, for the sole purpose of alleviating, in any way whatsoever, the conditions of people who were outcasts, outlawed by society, for the sole purpose of protecting them against the arbitrariness of the pitiless police system—this was heroism the like of which is rarely to be found even in the history of Russian literature.

And Chekhov accomplished this exploit quietly and secretly, his only concern being that outsiders should not regard it in any way as an exploit.

Unfortunately, he attained his objective. There are whole books about Chekhov which do not even mention this Sakhalin period of his life.

Chekhov set off for Sakhalin not as the empowered representative of some organization, not on a special assignment for some influential, rich newspaper, but on his own account, without any letters of recommendation, simply as an ordinary mortal without any privileges whatsoever.

When, drenched to the skin and after having walked several miles over a vile road up to his knees in water, he arrived at a small house together with a certain general, the general changed into dry clothes and was given a bed, but Chekhov had to lie down on the bare floor in clothes which were soaked through and through.

And on Sakhalin Island itself he undertook so much work that of all the people there, including those serving sentences, he was the hardest worked person for the several months he spent at the place.

In collecting material for his future book Chekhov tackled a monstrously difficult job: taking a census of the entire population inhabiting an island which is twice the size of Greece. It was an undertaking worthy of a whole staff of workers. He did it all by himself, without any assistance, going from house to house, from one prison cell to another.

Is it any wonder that his journey to that convict isle finally undermined his health, already none too robust? Added to this, he caught cold on the way back and began to cough much more violently than ever before. His premature death can undoubtedly be explained by the fact that during this period, when he could still have treated his tuberculosis, which had only just set in, he spent several months under such insufferable difficult conditions that they would have put a healthy person on his back. Furthermore, the trip ruined him financially, for he spent all his own money on it. His drivers alone he paid double and triple what he should have paid and incidental travelling companions robbed him right and left. After this journey he found himself hard up for a long time, and even four years later he wrote:

"I spent more time and money on that trip and that work than I'll be able to make up in a decade."

And when, some time later, he accidentally found himself in a solitary, remote place under pernicious, exhausting conditions, he wrote a letter to Gorky which contained a rather tardy complaint:

"How terrible it is here—something like my trip to Siberia!"

But even when he returned from Sakhalin, coughing, and with heart trouble, he never once struck a heroic pose. Indeed, he talked of the journey in his usual ironical tone.

"Yes, Sashechka," he wrote his elder brother, "I've travelled all round the world, and if you want to know what I saw, read Krylov's fable The Curious. What butterflies, insects, flies and roaches!"

Not one of his countless friends and acquaintances, literally not a single one, had the remotest conception of his purpose in making his journey to that penal island. Even Suvorin, who at that time was one of those closest to him, even he, in friendly banter, sent him the following telegram to Irkutsk:

"Don't brag. Stanley's a long way ahead of you yet."

His brother Alexander, an irrepressible wit, congratulated him immediately upon his return:

"Globe-trotting brother, I've heard that you've been roaming all over the world, that you've lost the last shred of mind you possessed and have returned more crazy even than when you left."

Critics stubbornly refused to take notice of the fact that in Sakhalin Island, as in his other books, Chekhov revealed himself in his true colours as a champion of the happiness of the people. While still preparing for Sakhalin he wrote: "Not more than twenty-five or thirty years ago Russians made a study of Sakhalin and did amazing things, things that make one feel able to venerate the name of man." Is there any need to prove that Chekhov himself belonged to that group of Russians?

Burenin commented on his trip with the following harmless banter:

> A talented scribe by the name of A. Chekhov
> To Sakhalin Isle on a journey did set off.
> For days without end 'midst its cliffs he did blunder
> In search of the Muse—Inspiration—to dun her.
> He sought high and low, but the Muse remained hidden.
> Then swiftly he turned back the way he had ridden.
> Our tale's simple moral's as old as creation:
> Stray not too far for your art's inspiration.

All of these remarks contain much raillery but not one iota of admiration for this great achievement of Chekhov's. Much later his close friends still continued their good-natured jokes on the subject. Replying to one of Suvorin's letters which we do not possess, Chekhov twice mentions the fact that Suvorin ridicules his Sakhalin essays, their "seriousness", "learnedness", "dryness". And Chekhov remonstrates:

"Of course there's no sense in printing *Sakhalin* in a magazine . . . but published as a little book I think it might be of use. In any case, your ridicule is to no purpose."

At the time, however, the "little book" did prove to be of no purpose, and evoked no public comment. It must be said, to the shame of the society of those days, that Chekhov's *Sakhalin Island*, which was published several years after his return and which had entailed such sacrifices on his part, remained almost unnoticed in the literary world. Only the periodical *Books of the Week* observed acidly that it was absolutely futile for Chekhov to spend his energy on work which an ordinary journalist could write. Only one person, Skabichevsky—and four years after its appearance at that—mentioned it along with a number of other works dealing with the same subject, not even paying Chekhov's book the tribute of a separate review.

Not until Chekhov was already dead did a famous scientist, Professor Mikhail Chlenov, declare in the Moscow University newspaper that, in the future, *Sakhalin Island* "will serve as a model for works of this nature, when a department of ethnographical medicine, which we need so much, is opened up".

During Chekhov's lifetime, however, university medical men merely shrugged their shoulders when it was mentioned that the author merited a scientific degree for this "exemplary work". "Who? Yesterday's Antosha Chekhonte? Impossible!"

It must frankly be admitted, however, that while the book was conceived with the noblest of aims, it is immeasurably weaker than any other of Chekhov's works, for it lacks the most important thing—Chekhov himself. Throughout he never lets himself go as an artist, but pitilessly suppresses his gift of description. One would never guess that it was written by a master who, at that very time, was capable of moving his readers to tears. We look forward to every new page, hoping that Chekhov will drop the cloak of the scientist and will at last begin to speak in his own magic language—the language of full-blooded, significant images—and that we will then not only understand, but also feel until it hurts, all the insidious horrors of the seemingly orderly, everyday life on Sakhalin Island. But there is never an intimation of this. He was at the zenith of his powers then, and there is no doubt whatever that he could have written a book of overwhelming force, but, as has happened more than once in Russian literature, he "stepped on the throat of his own song" and strangled it.

Even so, the book is full of Chekhov's main theme—the crying senselessness and futility of the suffering which one group of people, either individually or collectively, for some reason or other, inflicts on others. With irrefutable clarity, with facts and figures, he reveals, slowly, methodically, earnestly, thoroughly, the stupidity of Tsarist penal servitude, of the brutish humiliation by the propertied and the well-fed of the social outcasts. And what is characteristic of the writers and critics of those days is that they not only showed no inclination to support Chekhov's theme, if only within the limits permitted by the censors, but on the contrary, and despite every evidence to the contrary, they continued to declare Chekhov an unprincipled writer without ideas and indifferent to the interests and needs of Russian society.

When the book was finally written—it took him a year—Chekhov dropped all reference to his Sakhalin trip, whether in conversation or in his letters. It was as though the trip had never taken place. In all the three volumes of his correspondence with his wife, *Sakhalin Island* is mentioned only once, and then only in passing, merely as the title of a book.

"There is nothing to indicate that he liked to recall that trip," Potapenko says. "At any rate, although I spent quite a few days with him, I never heard him recount a single episode about that particular world."

Even on the rare occasions when he had to provide autobiographical information about himself for the press, he ascribed very little significance to his journey to Sakhalin, and there was hardly a word to suggest its difficulties and hardships.

IV

Scarcely anybody who ever met Chekhov has failed, when speaking of him, to mention one profoundly national characteristic of his; this was his deep-rooted dislike of self-glorification and boasting. It was almost impossible to believe that he, who was revered by the entire country, could remain so indifferent to his own fame.

Indeed, it seemed as though Chekhov had deliberately set himself the task of effacing his own ego and of carefully avoiding the danger of inhibiting anyone by his own achievements, his own superiority.

When a complete collection of his works was being prepared for publication, he asked the publisher to do him the special favour of *not* including either his portrait or his biography in the edition, and he insisted on having his way. His biography was omitted, although long established tradition demanded that a biography of the author should be placed at the beginning of the first volume of a complete collection of works.

"In Paris the well-known sculptor, Bernstam, wanted to model me but I refused to give in," he told Jordanov in 1899.

In the pictures where he is shown together with other people, he is almost always, with only two or three exceptions, to be found in the shade, somewhere behind somebody, or, at best, off to one side. He could not bear the idea of sitting down near the centre of a group, or of being its central figure. All his life he strictly observed that austere rule which, when still a youth, he had set both himself and his weak-willed brother, admonishing him: "Real talent always keeps in the shade, among the crowd, as far from the spotlight as it can get."

It would not be amiss if young writers made a thorough study of Chekhov's life and sought to fashion their own behaviour accordingly. His life is first and foremost a textbook on modesty in writers.

In January 1900 the Academy of Sciences elected him an honorary member.* That was the highest honour a writer could attain in those days. But he appeared to ignore it completely. Only once did he jokingly sign a letter to some member of his family, "Academician Toto". And when he was on the point of entering his title in his wife's passport, but . . .

"At first I wanted to make you the wife of an honorary academician, but then I decided that it was far pleasanter to be the wife of a doctor."

---

* Later Chekhov resigned his honorary fellowship as a protest when the Tsar annulled the election of Gorky to honorary membership of the Academy.

And he wrote "wife of a doctor"—since the word "physician" was the most unnoticeable, commonplace title; he would not change it for any other.

He never gave public readings of his works on the stage, or even before small groups of friends. At the theatre he usually sat in the last row.

There was only one condition he imposed on the library to which he presented thousands of books:

"Please don't mention my participation in library affairs to anyone."

And when the library asked him for a portrait of himself, he promised to send a portrait of Alphonse Daudet.

He was constantly worried lest he offend anyone by his own fame and superiority. Among his acquaintances was the writer, Vladimir Tikhonov, a man not without ability, but, compared to Chekhov, Tikhonov was one of the foothills of Mt. Elbras. Yet here is how Chekhov extended an invitation to Tikhonov to visit him:

"My very dear Vladimir Alexeyevich, I'm not going to invite you to the country to visit me, for that would be futile. You're as proud and haughty and arrogant as Nebuchadnezzar. Were the Prince of Coburg or the Egyptian Khedive to invite you, you would very likely accept, but an invitation from an insignificant Russian writer most probably evokes only a scornful smile. That's a pity. Your pride prevents you coming to see me, yet what excellent sour cream I have, what lamb, what cucumbers we'll have in May, and what radishes!"

To avoid offending an insignificant Russian writer by seeming to be overweening in his attitude towards him, Chekhov calls himself "insignificant" and lowers himself to Tikhonov's level as though he were not a Chekhov but a Tikhonov.

It was his habit, when talking to some third-rate writer, to say: "You and I," lest the others—Heaven forbid—might think Chekhov considered himself superior. "When Suvorin sees a bad play," he wrote to the same Tikhonov, "he hates the author, while you and I merely get annoyed and grumble; from this I conclude that Suvorin would make a good judge and a good bloodhound, whereas we (you, I, Shcheglov, and others) are, by nature, fit only to be defendants and hares."

This extreme delicacy often prompted him to ask forgiveness of people for things that could not possibly have given offence.

"Once, at dinner in Paris," he wrote to one of his rich friends, "you tried to persuade me to remain in Paris, and offered to lend me money, but I refused, and it seemed to me that this refusal of mine both grieved and angered you, and that when we parted you were rather cold. Perhaps I am mistaken. But if not, I want to assure you that I refused not because I did not want to borrow anything from you. . ."

Chekhov is, apparently, the only man who ever asked his friends to forgive him for not borrowing money from them!

V

I doubt if any of those who extolled Chekhov's gentleness, delicacy and modesty realized that in these native qualities could be seen what he himself called his "animal training".

To be "his own animal-trainer", to tame himself, to make moral demands of himself that were almost beyond anyone's power and to see to it that they were lived up to—this was the chief element of his life, and the role he loved above all others—the role of being his own educator. Only in this way did he attain that spiritual beauty of his, as the result of much persistent effort. An admission which he himself accidentally made has come down to us, to the effect that he had deliberately inculcated in himself one of the finest elements in his personality. When his wife wrote him that he had a soft, yielding character, he replied in a letter dated 1903:

"I must tell you that by nature my character is very harsh; I flare up easily, etc., etc., but I am accustomed to restraining myself, for no decent person should let himself go. The devil only knows what I used to do in the old days."

The story of Chekhov's life becomes all the more instructive when one realizes that this strong-willed man, who in his youth had done "the devil only knows what", had succeeded in suppressing his temper, in ridding himself of everything petty and base, and in developing in himself such delicacy and gentleness as no other writer of his generation was known to possess.

And his extreme modesty, his constant striving to remain in the shade, his wish to evade fame—these traits, too, were not innate in him but the result of his "animal training".

"I'm as ambitious as they make 'em," he admitted in one of his intimate letters. "I only pretended to be indifferent, but I was terribly excited," he wrote after the St. Petersburg performance of *Ivanov*. The way he received the celebrated failure of his play, *The Sea-gull*, in 1896 is evidence of how much his literary success really meant to him. "He was very sensitive about the success of his works," Suvorin says in his obituary notice of Chekhov, and in his diary he wrote: "Chekhov was very proud, and when I told him what I thought (about the reasons for the failure of *The Sea-gull*—K.C.) he listened to me impatiently. He could not think of that failure without being profoundly roused by it."

And so, when Chekhov scorned personal success, he was scorning something that had always attracted him. It would indeed have been strange if a man with such love of life, who was such a social creature, had remained indifferent to the charms and attractions of fame. I recall his earlier letters that include passages in which, unlike his Chekhovian self, he boasts of his successes and at times—again unlike Chekhov—he tries to bolster up his literary fame.

It is illuminating to recall how passionately, towards the end of his life, he attacked the ill-starred Nikolai Efros because this man—who had long been his admirer, a friend of his family, an enthusiast, and the chronicler of the Moscow Art Theatre—in recounting the contents of Chekhov's *The Cherry Orchard* in the press, made some slight (and wholly excusable) deviations from the text.

The fact that the reins in which he had held himself in check all his life were slackened towards the end, as a result of his illness, enables us to see even more clearly how severe had been his ever-vigilant control over himself.

Two writers who had the opportunity to observe him at closer range and for a longer period than any others—Shcheglov-Leontyev and Potapenko—both noted in their memoirs that Chekhov's greatness did not come tumbling down on him from the heavens.

"During that first period of buoyant youth and the rush of success," Shcheglov-Leontyev writes, "Chekhov, at times, manifested such unpleasant characteristics, such adolescent, light-minded arrogance and, I might even say, gaucherie. . . The third time he came to St. Petersburg, however, there was no sign whatever of such harsh dissonances in his character."

According to Potapenko, many who have written about Chekhov have pictured him as a "being void of flesh and blood, a self-righteous person who is beyond life, who has rid himself of all human weaknesses, a man without passions, who never goes astray, who never makes mistakes". No, Chekhov was not a saint, not a self-righteous goody-goody, and his attractive spiritual qualities were, as Potapenko observed, achieved at "the price of painful inner struggle, the laurels of a hard-earned victory".

Springing from petty bourgeois surroundings which he hated with the burning hatred that later filled all his books, he reached the conviction, when still a youth, that only that man who had cleansed his own house of purulent matter could struggle victoriously against the philistine degeneration of the human soul. And as there were two chief vices in every philistine soul—the lust to outrage the weak and the desire to abase oneself before the strong—he determined to rid himself of them completely. The first of these vices, in all the countless forms that it assumes—insolence, arrogance, boastfulness, haughtiness, superciliousness, presumptuousness, overbearing pride—he burnt out of himself as with a red-hot poker. The second vice was much more difficult to manage. Heroic will-power was required of him before he could develop such splendid pride within himself—he, a man of humble birth, brought up in a parsimonious environment where people bowed before every cockade and grovelled before every purse. He himself refers to this in a celebrated letter to his friend Suvorin :

"Write a story about how a young man (that is, Chekhov—K.C.), son of a serf, a former shopkeeper, a choirboy, a *gymnasia* and university student, brought up to respect rank, to kiss the priest's hand, to prostrate himself before the thoughts of others, giving thanks for every mouthful of bread, flogged repeatedly, going to the pupils he tutored without goloshes, a fellow who gets into scrapes, torments animals, and loves to dine with his rich relatives, who is hypocritical before God and man without reason, merely through the realization of his own insignificance—write how this young man slowly but surely strangles the slave in himself, until he awakes, one beautiful morning, feeling that no longer does servile blood course through his veins, but the blood of a real man."

It is an astonishing admission and no wonder that all who write about Chekhov quote the passage and smack their lips in enjoyment of it.

For it speaks of a miracle.

One would imagine that if you, in childhood, had been inoculated with the virus of slavish cringing before everyone who was even slightly more powerful than yourself, if you, like—as Chekhov put it— every "two legs" of that epoch, were brought up in a spirit of servility, if, back in your parents' home, you were taught to grovel before the rich and mighty, to flatter and agree with them, then, no matter how much you might try to crush that habit of toadying, willy-nilly it would show itself to the end of your days, in your gestures, in your smiles, in the intonations of your voice. The fact that Chekhov succeeded is evidence of another rare quality of his. I will return to this later.

But for the moment I want to emphasize the fact that Chekhov was strikingly successful—where so many have failed—in completely freeing his mind of all traces of servility, obsequiousness, subservience, self-abasement and fawning.

A sense of one's own personal dignity appears to be a hereditary quality, something that cannot be acquired by training alone; in any case, although dulled by the influence of a philistine environment, it was inherent in Chekhov from his earliest childhood (as is evidenced to no small degree in the letters and reminiscences of his older brother). Yet colossal will-power was required to reduce that philistine influence to nought.

Not in a single one of his numerous letters can one find anything that even hints at grovelling before others, not one single fawning word designed to procure some favour for himself. In the very first letter of his that has come down to us, written with rather childlike *naïveté*, he preaches self-respect to his younger brother.

"There's one thing I don't like: Why do you call yourself 'your insignificant, inconspicuous kid-brother'? You admit your insignificance? Not to everyone, brother. Not all Mishas need be alike. Do you know where to admit your insignificance? Before God, perhaps, before wisdom, beauty, Nature, but not before people. When among people, you must recognize your own worth. Why, you're not a scoundrel but an honest person, aren't you? Then respect yourself as an honest fellow and know that an honest fellow is not a nonentity."

And several years later he addressed his elder brother in the same way, demanding of him self-respect and lofty, human pride—when this brother, who was living with a woman without the sanction of the Church, fawned upon his devout father at every opportunity in order to win him over to a favourable attitude towards his irregular union.

It is characteristic of Chekhov that while he was free and easy with many, especially in his youth, and although he spoke of his plays rather scornfully and called his stories trifles, yet no one dared to take liberties with him. Despite his great considerateness for people, he was never afraid of offending anyone if that person wounded his self-respect in even the slightest degree.

In 1888 a certain critic, who, though lacking in talent yet had considerable influence, and who had written a lot about Chekhov, wrote and asked him to come and see him, certain that the young writer would be eager to come and meet the man who could make certain that his work received the most favourable review in the most influential Moscow newspaper. But Chekhov, always so ready to see anybody, flatly refused to go. The critic was offended, whereupon Chekhov wrote to one of their mutual friends that he considered it an absurd grievance:

D

"In the first place, I couldn't visit him because I don't know him," he wrote. "Secondly, I don't visit people towards whom I feel indifferent, any more than I attend anniversary dinners in honour of writers I haven't read. Thirdly, the time has not yet come when I must go to Mecca to pay homage."

No one would class the feeling that prompted this letter as meekness. On the contrary, the letter reflected a militant, fighting spirit. This always flared up in Chekhov whenever he had occasion to protect his honour as a writer. He preferred to be uncivil and sharp rather than to flatter, in the slightest degree, the great and the powerful.

In this respect he would permit himself no compromise whatever, and he entertained wholehearted scorn for those writers who were unable to develop such pride. For instance, when Yassinsky, pretending nothing at all had happened, began to work on the newspaper in whose pages Victor Burenin had given him such a roasting, Chekhov wrote of Yassinsky:

"By his appearance in *Novoye Vremya* he has spat in his own face. There's not a cat in the world that has ever mocked a mouse the way Burenin ridiculed Yassinsky. . . There is a limit to every outrage, and in Yassinsky's place I would not only not show my face at *Novoye Vremya*, but not even on Malaya Italyanskaya Street" (where the editorial offices of the newspaper were located).

Or take Chekhov's relations with Suvorin, which extended over a period of many years. At that time Suvorin was a force and a power —he was the publisher of the newspaper with the largest circulation in Russia, a man with immense influence and, furthermore, exceedingly rich. Chekhov and he became close friends. Of course there were the enemies, the false friends, and the envious ones who persistently declared that Chekhov derived all kinds of benefits, and especially money, from this friendship with Suvorin, for at that time no one cultivated Suvorin's friendship disinterestedly.

To people who did not know Chekhov, this calumny might have had a semblance of truth, for Suvorin liked to play the Maecenas. His purse was always open for writers who hobnobbed with him. Maslov got piles of money out of him; so did Skalkovsky, Yassinsky, Hippius, Prince Baryatinsky, Morezhkovsky, Potapenko. In quite a short time he gave no less than 18,000 rubles to Amfiteatrov alone. And so it seemed very plausible that his favourite colleague and crony also enjoyed his liberality.

At the very beginning of their friendship Suvorin, seeing that Chekhov was hard up, offered him a generous advance, but Chekhov, who was hypersensitive on this score, wrote him the following letter in order to put a stop to it once and for all:

"I'll tell you frankly, and this is between ourselves : When I began to work on *Novoye Vremya*, I felt I had discovered El Dorado and promised myself I would write as often as possible in order to earn as much as possible—there's nothing wrong with that. But when you and I got to know each other better, and I began to feel you were one of my friends, all my suspicions were aroused and my work for the paper, for which I was paid, of course, lost its real value for me. . . I began to fear lest our relations might be spoiled by someone thinking I needed you not as a person, but as a publisher."

The situation seemed to be a very common one : the proud pauper cherishing his spiritual independence refuses to take advantage of his rich friend. But before three years had elapsed these financial relations between the proud pauper and his wealthy friend had taken a paradoxical, almost incredible, turn. It happened that it was not Chekhov who enjoyed the generosity of his rich friend, as journalistic circles of the time so persistently declared, but it was the rich friend who kept deriving more and more money from his friendship with Chekhov.

For about a dozen years Suvorin enjoyed what might almost be called exclusive rights as Chekhov's publisher. It would probably be unfair to say, in this instance, Suvorin himself tried to make any exorbitant profits from his client, but the publishing house itself was fundamentally so dishonest that during all the years when it published his *Kashtanka*,* *Sullen People*, *Muzhiks*, *Children*, and other stories, Chekhov received at most half of what he could have got from any other publisher—especially if one takes into account the fact that Suvorin, with the laxity characteristic of him at the time, was very negligent in his publication of books and turned them out with such great delays that it virtually spelt ruin for the author.

This situation finally forced itself even on Chekhov's attention, but he preferred to remain Suvorin's Maecenas than have Suvorin his. The friendship not only entailed a considerable financial loss for him, but it also caused him serious moral harm, for Suvorin's paper was openly reactionary then. However, when the publishing house was dissolved Chekhov had the satisfaction of knowing that he alone had succeeded in preserving his pride to the end, in the atmosphere of servile toadying, careerism and squabbling over seniority which then engulfed Suvorin.

"Chekhov was a man of pride," the dramatic critic A. Kugel says in his reminiscences. According to Kugel, the author of *The Sea-gull* refused to have anything to do with him, inasmuch as Kugel was

---

* Meaning *Chestnut*, the name of a puppy.

considered the "terror of the theatres", before whom actors and playwrights trembled.

Chekhov demanded this same pride of others. "Why, why does Sava Morozov receive aristocrats?" he asked indignantly in one of his later letters. "They merely eat their fill and then laugh at him as at a savage. I'd drive those beasts out at the end of a stick."

VI

It would indeed have been strange if this man, in educating himself, had not tried to re-educate others. He loved to teach people about him and he believed, with astonishing artlessness, in the power of precepts and sermons, or, as he put it, "reprimands".

When flirting with the beautiful Lika, he included the following stricture among the joking and nonsense he wrote to her: "You have absolutely no inclination for real work. That's why you're ill, why you look so sour and complain, why all you girls are good for nothing except giving penny lessons. . . Next time don't make me mad with your laziness, and please don't try to justify yourself. Where it's a matter of urgent work or a pledged word, I won't allow such things."

Even in a love-letter to his wife, whom he had just married, he wrote:

"It's impossible, impossible that way, darling. You must be wary of injustice. One must be scrupulous as regards justice, absolutely scrupulous."

These "impossibles" and "musts" were irrefutable commandments which he imposed upon those who were close to him, for he always imposed similar ones upon himself. Even when he lay on his death-bed, he tried to instil in Shcheglov-Leontyev the elementary feelings of self-respect and pride:

"Messrs. Burenin and Co. worry you, but why, why do you hang around them, that is, why do you make yourself dependent upon them? Why don't you leave if you despise them? Don't lower yourself, dear Jean, don't demean your own gifts. . . Be free, make yourself free. . ."

This began when he was still "Antosha Chekhonte". It is difficult to conceive that at the very time when he referred to himself, in his letters, as the most flippant of all fiction writers, as an author who was trying to "concoct some fiddle-faddle", at a time when he was staging "bacchanalia" in his home and, as Shcheglov put it, his whole flat "shook with laughter", he was simultaneously carrying on the difficult, herculean job of re-educating his family.

His brother Mikhail recalls that such "harsh, curt comments as 'that's not true,' 'you've got to be fair,' 'you mustn't lie,' and others suddenly began to appear in our family, expressions unknown to me before."

From the age of twenty, Chekhov became the breadwinner and head of his large family, which consisted of no less than four brothers, a sister, and his father. His sister readily lent herself to his teachings. His father, a petty despot and an inveterate tyrant, at first was hard as flint in this respect, but even he in the end succumbed to Chekhov's influence.

However, things were more difficult when it came to his brothers. Alexander, who was a writer, and Nikolai, who was a cartoonist, were lazy louts and given to boozing; it was in vain that Chekhov tried to bring all his wiles and powers as a teacher to bear on them— they fled from him like cowards. Both squandered their talents hopelessly and came to bad ends. Their spiritual bankruptcy was a vivid illustration of what might have been the fate of their great brother had he not disciplined himself so well.

It is characteristic of him that his reprimands were almost always liberally "spiced" with jokes, so that his insistent injunctions were not dull or sanctimonious. His letters to his brother Alexander consisted, for the most part, of two elements which, at first glance, might seem incongruous in any pedagogical system: the most provocative witticisms and the most severe moral aphorisms. Chekhov always had a ready fund to draw on for these aphorisms, and at times they were most unexpected. For instance, when he learned that Alexander was gorging himself on certain southern dishes Chekhov admonished him:

"Don't eat that stuff, brother. Why, it's just filth, garbage. . . In any case, don't give Mosevna (Alexander's daughter) just any old food. At least teach her the aesthetics of the stomach. And speaking of aesthetics—don't take offence, my dear, but you ought to be a parent not simply in words. Teach by setting an example. . . A child is impressed first of all by external appearances, and you've let yourself go to the dogs. And there's another type of cleanliness. Don't swear aloud. You'll corrupt Katya (the maid—K.C.) and soil Mosevna's ear-drums with your lingo."

It is difficult to believe that this was a younger brother rebuking an older one. And when this older brother was already in his thirties his younger brother still kept striving to re-educate and ennoble him.

"The very first time I visited you," he wrote Alexander in 1889,

"I felt estranged by your appalling, absolutely uncalled-for attitude towards Natalia Alexandrovna (Alexander's wife) and the cook. Please excuse me for saying so, but to treat a woman like that, no matter who she may be, is unworthy of any decent, loving person !"

"I want you to remember," he continues in the same letter, "that despotism and lies killed your mother's youth. Despotism and lies spoiled our childhood to such a degree that it is sickening and terrible to recall it. Remember the horror and disgust we used to feel when father, at dinner-time, raised a row because the soup was over-salted, or called Mother a fool. . . Despotism is thrice criminal."*

Perhaps this constant preaching to some slight extent restrained the dissolute "Sashechka" (Alexander—K.C.), but Nikolai was altogether unmanageable.

"It's impossible to find anyone who is more of a balalaika-hound than our Nikolai," Chekhov lamented. "And what is worse—he's incorrigible. . . Nikolai . . . is squandering his time; a good, vigorous Russian talent is going to the dogs, and all for nothing."

Chekhov tried to save him, and wrote him letter after letter ; among them is one in which he outlines in detail his whole anti-philistine moral code. Although this letter has been quoted numerous times, I cannot refrain from including some of its most essential passages here, for it gives a clear picture of the discipline which Chekhov imposed on himself.

Like everyone who is a teacher by vocation, and who is eager to ennoble both himself and others, Chekhov was optimistic about the miraculous effect of education. His brother Mikhail recalls that during an argument with V. A. Wagner, a well-known zoologist, who served as the prototype of von Koren in *The Duel*, Chekhov hotly declared that upbringing was stronger than heredity, that by proper upbringing we can overcome even degenerate mental qualities, which, like fate, might be expected to predetermine human actions.

That is why, in 1886, he sent the rapidly degenerating Nikolai a letter containing a set of precepts which even now could serve as a course in practical ethics.

". . . You have but one fault," Chekhov writes. "It is due to the fact that you were extremely ill bred. Well-bred people, in my opinion, must adhere to the following conditions :

"(1) They have respect for man, and are therefore always forbearing, gentle, polite and compliant. They never create a rumpus because of a lost hammer or a lost indiarubber. When living with someone they

---

* This eliminates all doubt as to the autobiographical aspect of such a story as *Difficult People*.

don't act as though they were conferring a favour and when leaving they don't say: 'It's impossible to live with you!' They forgive both noise and cold, overdone meat and caustic remarks, and the presence of outsiders in their home.

"(2) They feel compassion not only for beggars and cats. Their hearts ache for things one doesn't see with the naked eye. . .

"(3) They respect other people's property, and so they pay their debts.

"(4) . . . They don't pose, but conduct themselves in public just as they do at home, and don't bluster in front of their lesser brethren. . . They are not garrulous and do not inflict their confidences on people who have not asked for them. . . Out of respect for the ear of others, they are often silent.

"(5) They do not humble themselves to arouse sympathy. They do not play upon the heart-strings of others in order to excite pity and be made a fuss of. They don't say: 'Nobody understands me!' or: 'I've wasted my efforts!' because all of this merely produces a cheap effect and is vulgar, stale and false. . .

"(6) They develop their aesthetic taste. They will not fall asleep in their clothes; they cannot stand a crack in the wall with bedbugs in it, or breathe foul air, or walk across a floor that has been spat on, or eat straight off a kerosene stove. They strive as far as possible to restrain and ennoble the sexual instinct. . . What they require of woman is not mere physical relief . . . nor yet a mind that expresses itself in the ability to prevaricate tirelessly. What they—and especially artists—require is freshness, charm, human feeling, the capacity to be not a bitch but a mother. . . They don't guzzle their vodka and don't sniff at cupboards, for they know they are not swine. They drink only when they are free, when the occasion presents itself. . ."

And so on.

"That's what well-bred people are like. It is not enough to have read *Pickwick* or to have learnt by heart a soliloquy from *Faust* in order to be well bred and not fall below the level of the circle in which one moves.

"What one needs is constant work, day and night, incessant reading, study and exercise of will. Every hour is precious. . .

"Have the courage to send it all to hell and make a decisive break once and for all. . . Pay us a visit, go on the water-wagon, relax and read for a bit . . . if it's only Turgenyev, whom you haven't read. . .

"And forget your vanity; you're not an infant. . . You'll be thirty soon! It's time!

"I'm expecting you . . . we're all expecting you. . ."

This letter throws much light on the remarkable educational method with the help of which Chekhov trained himself. This youthful moral code of his is remarkable enough; what is a thousand times more remarkable, however, is that Chekhov succeeded in subordinating his whole life to this code, and that he lived up to every one of the precepts laid down in this letter. These precepts did not remain on paper, as so often happens. Of course anyone can make exacting demands of himself, demands that almost defy fulfilment, but only one person in a million can, throughout the course of an entire life-time, live up to them without deviating. Only that man can do so who possesses an exceptionally firm character, an exceptionally powerful will.

At last I have come to the words: *powerful will*! Everything that has been said in this chapter hitherto has been said with the single aim of finally asserting this "unorthodox" truth about Chekhov, and of proving it beyond any shadow of doubt, so that even dullards will realize that the basis of Chekhov's personality was his powerful, remarkably persistent will. Such a will is literally expressed in every incident of his life and, first and foremost—as we have seen—in the fact that when, in youth, he set himself a high and lofty ideal he imperiously subordinated his entire conduct to it. Russia has had many writers who were anxious to regulate their lives according to the dictates of their conscience—Gogol, Leo Tolstoy, Nekrasov, Nikolai Leskov, Gleb Uspensky, Garshin—and we admire their striving for a "correct", righteous life. But this moral achievement was at times beyond even their strength, and at times they simply grew weary and fell by the wayside. But this never happened to Chekhov: he had but to make this or that ruthless demand of himself, whatever it was that his conscience dictated to him, and he fulfilled it no matter what it cost him.

"I despise laziness, just as I despise weakness and sluggishness of the emotions," he said, speaking of himself. And we have just seen how when, at the end of the 'eighties, he came to the conclusion that Russia did not need his writing, he stopped writing abruptly at a time when his pen was bringing him fame, together with the material success of which he was in great need.

"I'm going—that's settled irrevocably!" he wrote Pleshcheyev on the eve of his Sakhalin journey—all his decisions bore the imprint of irrevocability.

"For him to decide to do something meant to do it," Ignati Potapenko says of him. An iron will was needed to suffer the unendurable torment of crossing a roadless Siberia, to keep him from turning back when he passed Tomsk, to make him travel those six thousand miles to the bitter end.

Chekhov's powerful will is seen more forcefully in his writing than in anything else.

What a tremendously free, independent spirit it required for him to be able, in defiance of those intolerably narrow-minded beings who called themselves liberals, to inscribe in bold letters on his unfurled standard:

"My Holy of Holies is the human body, health, wisdom, talent, inspiration, love and the most absolute freedom—freedom from the employment of violence and lies. . . I'm not a liberal nor a conservative, not an evolutionist nor a monk, nor am I an indifferentist. I hate lies and violence in all their forms and the secretaries of the consistory are equally repulsive to me as Notovich and Gradovsky. . ." "Phariseeism, stupidity and arbitrariness reign not only in merchants' homes and prisons; I see them in science, in literature, among the youth."

However we evaluate this challenge to his epoch, this revolt against its canons and everything it held sacred, we must admit that for such a defence of "absolute freedom" at that time, courage of a high order was necessary. Even if life later showed him that he was wrong in certain things, yet he had acquired the courage of his convictions and beliefs for all time and to the end of his days everyone regarded this as one of his most attractive qualities.

"Between you and me, you're the one and only free and independent person, you're a free Cossack* in mind and heart and body," Vladimir Tikhonov wrote to him in the 'eighties. "We're all fettered by routine, and can't rid ourselves of the joke."

Another fiction writer, King-Dedlov, also sensed this same quality in Chekhov. In 1903 he wrote him enviously:

"You have growing within you a quality that is most important for great talent—the courage to be truthful. You look life straight in the face without blinking, without turning your eyes away. You look at things with your own eyes, think with your own mind, regardless of what others say, and do not submit to the inner temptation to see what you would like to see."

Gorky, too, felt this and wrote him with astonishment and joy:

"It seems to me you are the first man I have ever met who is free and refuses to bow before anything."

And indeed, do we not feel this same freedom of will in him as a writer, as the creator of a new literary style! Nowhere, either in his conversations or in his letters, did he once call himself an innovator. Yet both as playwright and story-teller he effected a revolution and

---

* Cossack is a Tartar word meaning *free people.*

fought for the new forms he had created no less than Zola, for instance, fought for his. It would have been very easy for Chekhov to have satisfied the generally accepted taste in plays: he was a master of swift action and of all the current theatrical forms, but he imperiously rejected these forms and, without making the slightest compromise, won the right to his own style.

Everywhere, in everything he did, his powerful will remained unflinching to the end of his days.

Even if we knew nothing more about the last months of his life than what we could learn from his letters, about how, in spite of his terrible illness, he got up and sat at his desk, again and again, and in between attacks of diarrhoea, nausea, coughing, and spitting blood, he wrote with a hand that was growing cold, a hand "as white as gypsum", wrote his last play at the rate of two lines a day, with interruptions during which his manuscript lay untouched on his desk for weeks on end while he glanced at it from afar, pining and wasting away, but unable to add another word to it, and yet—he finished the work in the time he had set himself, overcoming his infirmity with his creative art—if we had but seen Chekhov in those months before his death, it would have been enough to convince us that here indeed was a man of heroic stature, a man with a powerful will. His composition of *The Cherry Orchard* under these conditions meant surmounting such superhuman difficulties as those he had encountered on his journey to the convict island; and once again he did not flinch or turn back. "Weakness and sluggishness of the emotions" was alien to him even on the brink of the grave.

VII

It may be asked: why do I seem to labour this point? Is it not obvious to everyone?

That is just what is so amazing—it is not. I could cover hundreds of pages with quotations from articles and booklets about Chekhov describing him as "weak-willed", "passive", "characterless", "inactive", "anaemic", "inert", "flabby", "impotent", "sluggish". All the criticism of the 'eighties, the 'nineties, and the nineteen hundreds kept hammering away at just this very point.

Even people who knew him personally, for instance, N. M. Yezhov (whom, by the way, Chekhov considered rather stupid), continually wrote of him:

"Like a man without character . . . He, like every weak person . . ."

And the last complete collection of his works, published in 1929, contains a lengthy and seemingly learned article in which the entire characterization of Chekhov presents just this very picture. It states in black on white, that inasmuch as Chekhov apparently belonged to some sort of "groundless, confusedly perplexed (?) group", he, both in his life and in his work, was a man "without will" (!) "passively sensitive" (?), "impressionable and with a weak nature" ! ! !

Even such a careful scholar as Professor N. K. Piksanov, in his foreword to the correspondence between Korolenko and Chekhov, writes—now in our own time—as though it were an established fact demanding no proof whatever, that Chekhov was "pathologically sluggish", that he "avoided meddling with the life about him" and that in this respect he was diametrically opposite to Korolenko. If the expression "pathologically sluggish" is supposed to mean that during his illness Chekhov became physically weak, then that is a condition common to all sick people, although Chekhov, as we have just seen, by the dogged exertion of his will-power, held in abeyance for a time even this terrible malady. If the label "pathologically sluggish" has been stuck on to Chekhov in the given instance as a general characteristic of his, I would counsel its being unstuck as quickly as possible, for it is in crying contradiction to *all* the facts of Chekhov's life.

It is my opinion that in the light of the facts which I have adduced, even those with strong, preconceived notions will at last cease to maintain that Chekhov had a weak character. If, however, there are still any who would like to dispute the point, I am ready to suggest a subject for discussion which will have a further bearing on the matter ; let them find in the Russian literature of those days at least one person who possessed an equally phenomenal will. One must indeed be blind not to see that during all these forty years Chekhov's will was his dominating quality, a quality that set him apart from all other Russian writers of the 'eighties.

It is customary to declare, quite arbitrarily, of Chekhov's epoch that it was one of complete sluggishness, sickliness, numbness, and stagnation of the masses of intellectuals. This is true, but it is only partly true : In Russia there could never be complete sluggishness. We must not forget that it was these very eighties of the past century that produced such fighters as Miklukha-Maklai, Przhevalsky, Alexander Ulyanov and—Chekhov.

The very compactness of his work, those steely frameworks which give his short stories more solidity than many a novel, his mastery of style, the manner in which he boldly and unerringly disposes of his material—all these are suggestive of one thing—power.

The human will, as the greatest force which is capable of fabulously transforming our life and for ever destroying its "leaden abominations", as Gorky puts it, is the central theme of all Chekhov's work, and the unusual wariness which he exercised with regard to all forms of injuries and fractures to and dislocations of that will, as reflected in his work, is explained by the very fact that he himself was a man of enormous will-power, a man who subordinated all his desires and acts to his unflinching will. To sum up, I have proceeded from the firm conviction that the inner meaning of the underlying Chekhovian theme—fated clashes between strong-willed and weak-willed people —becomes much clearer to us if we master the idea that his own entire life was governed by this very theme.

Chekhov's theme of the struggle between human will and the lack of will-power is the basic theme of his epoch. It was the very fact that Chekhov's personal theme proved to be an adequately social one that made him the most significant writer of his generation.

AN AFTERTHOUGHT

Three writers, utterly unlike each other, all of whom had known Chekhov at totally different times, have expressed themselves in one and the same way about Chekhov's personal appearance.

Peter Sergeyenko, a schoolfellow of Chekhov's in Taganrog and who also met him frequently in Moscow later, noted in his memoirs that in his youth Chekhov looked like a "pleasant Russian lad".

Vladimir Korolenko, who knew Chekhov much later, literally said the very same thing about him:

"In spite of Chekhov's undeniable refinement, his face had something in it which reminded you of a simple-hearted village lad."

And Alexander Kuprin, who became acquainted with Chekhov at a time when the disease he was suffering from held him in the throes of death, expressed himself in the very same way:

"There was something so simple and modest about him, something so extraordinarily Russian and national—in his face, his speech, the expressions he used."

Gorky refers to a conversation with Leo Tolstoy, in which the latter, after commenting very harshly on certain writers, turned to Chekhov and said gently:

"Now you—you are Russian! Yes, very, very Russian!"

And smiling affectionately, he put his arm round Chekhov's shoulders.

These Russian national characteristics must have been very striking indeed if even Balmont inscribed in a book he presented to Chekhov:

"To an artist with a genuinely Russian soul."

The following words of Sergeyenko's are a fitting commentary to this laconic inscription:

"All his actions and especially his writings are imbued with the youthful soul of the Russian people, with all its poetry and humour. . . Outwardly Chekhov was a typical example of a Russian peasant. It is a rare village where you will not find a peasant who looks like Chekhov, who has Chekhov's facial expression, and Chekhov's smile."

Although Chekhov was born in the South, near the Sea of Azov, and often jokingly called himself a "Khokhol", his mother and father were Russians, from the central regions. Chekhov himself, an out-and-out Moscovite, was typically Russian in all his tastes and habits. His simplicity, his hatred of pose and affectation, his modest, quiet,

61

unostentatious heroism and his heartfelt, deeply human talent—all these qualities of his were national, Russian qualities. That is why in November 1941—not long after the outbreak of the Patriotic War—Joseph Stalin mentioned Chekhov's name as one of the most glorious and beloved names of which the whole Russian people have every right to be proud.

K. C.

WHO'S WHO
OF PERSONS MENTIONED IN THE TEXT

1. AMFITEATROV, Alexander—journalist, novelist and short-story writer.
2. ANTOKOLSKY—Russian sculptor, author of the statues "Ivan the Terrible", "Socrates", "Mephistopheles".
3. BALMONT, Konstantin—poet (symbolist), translator of Marlowe, Shelley, Edgar Allan Poe and Walt Whitman.
4. BALUKHATY—scholar in the field of literature and authority on Chekhov.
5. BARYATINSKY, Prince Vladimir—journalist, playwright.
6. BERNSTAM, Leopold—Russian sculptor and portraitist, whose permanent residence was Paris.
7. BILIBIN, Victor—humorist, writer of vaudeville skits.
8. BOBORYKIN, Peter—author of many novels reflecting the intellectual life of Russian society during the second half of the 19th century.
9. CHEKHONTE, Antosha—the pseudonym of Chekhov's younger days.
10. EFROS, Nikolai—dramatic critic, historian of the Moscow Art Theatre.
11. FOFANOV, Konstantin—lyric poet, forerunner of the symbolists.
12. GARSHIN, Vsevolod—fiction writer, author of tales about the intellectuals of the 'seventies.
13. GILYAROVSKY, Vladimir—newspaper reporter.
14. GOLTZEV, Victor—professor of law, journalist, critic, editor of the monthly, *Russkaya Mysl* (Russian Thought).
15. GRADOVSKY, Grigory—quasi-liberal journalist.
16. HIPPIUS, Zinaida—poetess, novelist, critic of the school of symbolism.
17. JORDANOV—municipal head of the city of Taganrog.
18. KING-DEDLOV—fiction writer, author of travelogues.
19. KNIPPER, Olga—Chekhov's wife, actress of the Moscow Art Theatre.

20. KOROLENKO, Vladimir—short-story writer, journalist of the radical camp; was exiled to Siberia under Tsar Alexander III; author of numerous stories on the life of exiles and those sentenced to penal servitude.

21. KOVALEVSKY, Maxim—lawyer, sociologist, author of *The Social Structure of England, Origin of Modern Democracy*.

22. KUGEL, Alexander—dramatic critic.

23. KUPRIN, Alexander—short-story writer, known for his tales about the life of the Russian soldier and officer during the last decades of Tsarism.

24. LEIKIN, Nikolai—humorist, publisher and editor of a comic weekly in St. Petersburg.

25. LESKOV, Nikolai—fiction writer, author of the novel *Soboryane* and a number of stories on the life of the Russian clergy.

26. MASLOV, Alexei—writer about the life of military circles.

27. MEREZHKOVSKY, Dmitry—historian, philosopher, novelist and poet.

28. MIKHAILOVSKY—sociologist and literary critic, author of articles, *Struggle for the Personality, What is Progress?*, and others.

29. MIKLUKHA-MAKLAI—traveller, explorer of New Guinea and Polynesian islands.

30. MOROZOV, Savva—Moscow millionaire and patron of the arts.

31. NEMIROVITCH-DANCHENKO, Vladimir—playwright, novelist, producer and (with Konstantin Stanislavsky) founder of the Moscow Art Theatre.

32. NOTOVICH, Ossip—editor and publisher of the St. Petersburg liberal newspaper *Novosti* (The News).

33. PLESHCHEYEV, Alexei—poet of the radical camp; in connection with the Petrashevsky case was sentenced to serve as a rank-and-file soldier in exile.

34. PLEVAKO, Fyoder—Moscow lawyer, called "Moscow Zlatoust" (golden-mouthed).

35. POLONSKY, Jacob—poet and novelist, one of the finest poets after the Pushkin pleiad.

36. POTAPENKO, Ignati—author of tales and novels chiefly about the life of the village clergy.

37. POTEMKIN, Prince Grigory—favourite of Catherine II.

38. PRZHEVALSKY—explorer of Central Asia, traveller.

39. SEMIRADSKY, Sergei—painter of the academic school, author of paintings of ancient Greek and Roman life.

40. SERGEYENKO, Peter—writer, Chekhov's schoolmate, friend of Leo Tolstoy.

41. SHCHEGLOV-LEONTIEV—fiction writer and playwright.

42. SHCHEPKINA-KUPERNIK, Tatyana—poetess, short-story writer, modern translator of Shakespeare.
43. SHCHUKIN, Sergei—Russian priest.
44. SKABICHEVSKY—literary critic of the liberal camp.
45. SKALKOVSKY—mining engineer, journalist.
46. SLEPTSOV, Vasili—novelist, short-story writer, mainly about the life of peasants and urban middle-class; one of the forerunners of Chekhov.
47. SUVORIN, Alexei—journalist, playwright, short-story writer, founder of a large publishing house, editor and publisher of the reactionary newspaper *Novoye Vremya* (New Times).
48. TERPIGOREV, Sergei—pseudonym Sergei Atava; author of novels and stories about the degeneration of the nobility.
49. TIKHONOV, Alexander—modern Soviet writer, author of memoirs of Leo Tolstoy, Chekhov and Gorky.
50. TIKHONOV, Vladimir—fiction writer and playwright.
51. ULYANOV, Alexander—brother of Lenin, revolutionary, executed by Tsar Alexander III.
52. USPENSKY, Nikolai—author of numerous sketches on the life of the Russian village.
53. YASSINSKY, Yeronim—fiction writer.
54. YEZHOV, Nikolai—journalist.